What people are saying about CEOFlow...

"The CEOFlow live events are a great venue to discuss, with other people who can really relate – other CEOs – how to keep the real life stress and pressures of being a CEO from overwhelming your life. CEOFlow will grow into something big, a movement."

- Deva Hazarika, CEO, ClearContext

"Working with Aaron Ross has been nothing short of amazing! His methods applied to our sales organization helped us produce a profitable and scalable new stream of predictable revenue. We saw at least 40+% new business growth. The best part is, we had a blast while doing it!"

– Michael Stone, VP Sales, WPromote
(#1 ranked Search Marketing Firm on the Inc. 500)

"Aaron is the quintessential example of how great leaders can be if they set aside their egos, create a clear and bold vision, and empower their people to execute like mini-CEOs. I took over the team that Aaron created at Salesforce.com and I've been amazed by his leadership in building a solid foundation set for explosive and sustainable success. Thanks Aaron, you've made me look mighty good around here!"

- Ryan Martin, Director of New Business, Salesforce.com

"You are doing good helping people Aaron – your work will not go unnoticed – sharing and helping others is a true talent of yours."

- Ryan Born, CEO, AudioMicro

"The companies I've seen that have followed Aaron's advice have outperformed. What more can I say?"

- Tim Connors, General Partner, US Venture Partners

"Aaron has an amazing ability to assess, guide, and teach CEOs how to shift their approach to business to help them create more predictable revenue, a sales staff that runs itself as a sales machine, and to reduce stress and increase freedom in their lives. It's been my honor to work with him and witness the changes he helps others bring forth."

- Onna Young, Partner, PebbleStorm

"Your program has been inspirational. It's motivating and refreshing to shift my perspective from thinking that the corporate way is what one has to put up with in order to succeed. I feel a sense of freedom now that I'm on this path."

- Katrina Wong, PebbleStorm participant

"Aaron Ross is a wonderfully calm presence for me as I sort out my pulled-in-too-many-directions life of a business owner. When we speak he reminds me of using peace and joy as my directional device; compass. I know deeply that we are supposed to love work and have so much fun with it while making the money we want. In order to achieve this, he helps me to focus and prioritize. If you want to have a high quality life that is led by your heart Aaron is very helpful."

- Carenna Willmont, CEO, Whole Human Financial

"After attending my first CEOFlow gathering, I realized many of us CEOs face remarkably similar core issues. Better yet: the experience and advice from one entrepreneur is incredibly timely and relevant to another. There's nothing better than having a conversation with a group of bright, motivated leaders to focus in on what makes a company great."

- Andrei Stoica, Founder, ConnectAndSell

"There is something extraordinary that happens when smart business leaders sit down to talk about their ideas for transforming business, and Aaron Ross is a master at guiding these conversations to help find the real gems. I think a best-selling business book could come out of every one of these events — wish I had the time to write one of them"

- John Girard, CEO, Clickability

"I feel more and more honored that you are including me in something so fantastic. My compliment of the day for you: You make me feel calmer, more peaceful and more confident – so far, every time I have spoken with you. "Thank you …a thousand times…thank you. Your contribution to the enjoyment I experienced with my team is invaluable."

– Amy Applebaum, CEO, Bootcamp for Your Mind

"Aaron's one of the leading thinkers of the Sales 2.0 movement. I am inspired by Aaron's vision, amazed by his creativity and thankful for his counsel."

- Daniel Zamudio, CEO, Playboox

"Aaron has been a great advisor for AdaptAds. His 'cautiously but surely' approach matches that of AdaptAds. He brings invaluable learning experiences in terms of building a sales team. He's accessible, with the astutest of perspectives."

- Yogesh Sharma, CEO, AdaptAds

"Aaron Ross quickly grasped the issues and provided extremely helpful and creative ideas firmly rooted in his expertise about business growth. Most impressively, he did this with sensitivity to my personal motivations and comfort level. Thanks to Aaron, I now feel at ease moving my business to the national level."

- Klia Bassing, CEO, VisitYourself.net

"Aaron has a tremendously innovative sales process and methodology that helps companies grow their sales. He has a great philosophy I highly recommend all companies who are looking at increasing their revenues to look at Aaron for guidance."

- Josh Moreau, Sales Manager, X1

"Aaron is insightful, intelligent and highly dedicated to the missions he designs for his life. The focus, drive and determination Aaron demonstrates are admirable qualities that inspire. I would recommend Aaron to any company that is looking for a good person who is also a strong and formidable leader."

- Kim Santy, Founder, Soul Shui

"Aaron has always looked out for and fought for the best interests of people who work for him. Beyond that, he is smart, strategic, and can go just about anywhere he wants to go in this industry. He's a quality guy who I would jump to work with in the future."

- Brendon Cassidy, VP Sales, EchoSign

Dedication

Thank you Ricardo Semler, Dennis Bakke, Chip Conley, Yvon Chouinard, Tony Hsieh and all the other CEOs who not only created inspiring companies for themselves and their employees, but who have also taken the time to share their stories with us so that we could be inspired as well.

CEOFlow

Turn Your Employees Into Mini-CEOs

Aaron Ross

CEOFlow

ISBN 978-0-9843802-0-6

Publisher: PebbleStorm Press

Aaron Ross
PebbleStorm, Inc.
8605 Santa Monica Blvd, #39743
West Hollywood, CA 90069
(310) 751- 0656
Email: info@pebblestorm.com

www.CEOFlow.com

www.PebbleStorm.com

Limits of Liability and Disclaimer of Warranty

Warning – Disclaimer

Trust that little voice in your head that says,
'Wouldn't it be interesting if…' And then do it.

Duane Michals

ABOUT CEOFlow

"Leaders don't create followers, they create more leaders."
~ *Tom Peters*

Do you feel like you or your employees are the bottleneck to your business's growth? Or that you work for your business, rather than having a business that works for you?

What if the secrets to both your success and loving your business were right under your nose? They are called YOUR EMPLOYEES!

CEOFlow is a system and community of CEOs that helps you free up a bunch of time and energy by turning your employees into mini-CEOs who run your business like high-level executives.

CEOFlow and this book are for you if you want to:

- Inspire your employees to care as much about your business as you do.
- Create an environment where your employees always do a great job without you having to push them.
- Make sure you have the right systems in place for your employees to generate predictable sales time and time again
- Ensure that your employees give your customers the level of service and care that your business promises.
- Get as much free time as you desire for family, travel, adventure, or just get away from the business to think and reflect on what's next for it or for you.

The examples, ideas, and case studies in this book will inspire you and show you what is possible. Others have created their ideal work lives within their own businesses. Why can't you?

CEOFlow Coaching & Programs

We have coaching and consulting programs to help you implement the enclosed CEOFlow principles and to meet other like-minded CEOs. Contact us to find out more.

CEOFlow Advisory Council

If you are interested in joining or have a nomination for the CEOFlow Advisory Council, please reach out. The board is a group of leaders who want to support the CEOFlow vision of work and to support each other.

As part of the advisory board, leaders get to meet other like-minded peers to share stories on what works and doesn't work. They enjoy early looks at new material, discounts on programs and our live events, and access to myself and my team as well as other benefits.

Do You Have A Story To Share?

After reading this book and trying out some of the ideas, I would love to hear from you on what worked and what didn't work!

How To Contact Me

Write to info@pebblestorm.com.

(PebbleStorm is the parent company of CEOFlow.)

Jealously guard your enjoyment,

ABOUT THE AUTHOR

Aaron Ross is the founder of PebbleStorm. Our mission is to help 100 million people "make money through enjoyment" by showing them how to shift the way they do business and become more successful by making their work enjoyable and inspiring.

One of PebbleStorm's programs is CEOFlow, which helps leaders free up their time and energy by turning their employees into mini-CEOs who help them run the business like high-level executives.

Before PebbleStorm, Aaron Ross was an EIR (Entrepreneur-in-Residence) at Alloy Ventures, a $1 billion venture capital firm. Prior to Alloy, at Salesforce.com Aaron created a revolutionary sales lead generation process and team that helped increase Salesforce.com's recurring revenues by $100 million.

Aaron was CEO of LeaseExchange (now eLease.com), an online equipment leasing marketplace. As an entrepreneur, he has been featured in *Time, Business Week* and *The Red Herring*.

Aaron is also the cofounder of DataSalad ("Fresh B2B Marketing Data"), and on the advisory boards of Silicon Valley companies such as: Clickability, 4INFO, ConnectAndSell, AdaptAds, Playboox, AfterCollege, ExpertCEO and Flywheel Ventures.

"Build A Sales Machine" (www.BuildASalesMachine.com) is Aaron's business-to-business sales blog. He graduated from Stanford University with a degree in Environmental Civil Engineering. He is an Ironman triathlete, graduate of the Boulder Outdoor Survival School and volunteer mentor at SCORE, "Counselors to America's Small Business" and an avid motorcycle rider (www.MotoCEOs.com).

ABOUT THE SKETCHES

I do all the sketches myself. You can find out how I do them at:

www.PebbleStorm.com/category/sketches.

CONTENTS

Sketches

*"Leadership: the art of getting someone else
to do something you want done because he wants to do it."*

~ Dwight D. Eisenhower

1

Who Is Standing Up For You, The CEO?

While we complain about how painful work is for the everyday employee, we have to wonder about the daily stress of CEOs and how their job, your job, is often the most lonely and stressful in a company.

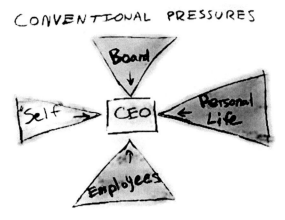

Don't turn your people into mini-CEOs just because making your people happier and more successful is the 'right' or popular thing to do – do it for selfish reasons.

Because, if you don't do it for selfish reasons, you won't stick with it.

Do it because it will make your business more successful. Your company's growth will be a direct reflection of how effective you are at turning your people into mini-CEOs.

Do it because it will make your work more fun and interesting: Isn't work more fun when you don't have to tell people what to do all the time and when the business works even while you're not participating?

Do it because you will make more money and have more time – whether you want to use it for more work or more play.

Do it because your life will be more fulfilling.

I have a vision for the future of how work can work differently. A future in which everyone enjoys their work and is more productive, successful, and inspire... and it starts with you, the CEO!

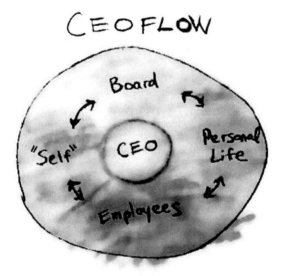

The CEO sets the example for the rest of the company. If the CEO is happy and inspired, they will manage through those values and the other employees will be more likely to be inspired. Likewise, if the CEO is stressed and controlling, they will manage by fear and that will also ripple out into the company's culture and to their markets and individuals or organizations they serve.

Why not use the inspiration and creativity of your entire company, rather than the limited energy of yourself and your favored executives?

I also have a vision for the kind of step-by-step system it takes to show CEOs how to develop self-managing teams and turn employees into mini-CEOs that help you run your company like high-level executives.

I want to inspire you to create a vision for yourself that is bigger, more exciting, freeing and fulfilling than what you have today. I also want to remind you that *your business is supposed to support & enhance how you want to live your life*, which is easy to forget about in the often-hectic pace of leading a company.

My goal is to awaken your imagination with stories from CEOFlow companies... The CEOFlow vision isn't just an abstraction; many company owners have figured out on their own how to turn their employees into mini-CEOs, and I practiced CEOFlow myself at Salesforce. com. CEOFlow is the systemization of how founders of companies that have created successful, profitable freedom cultures intuitively figured out how to turn their employees into mini-CEOs. I want to help more CEOs like yourself replicate their successes, in order to improve both your businesses and your life.

My goal with this book is to awaken your imagination with stories from management rules-breaking companies, to share an introduction to CEO-Flow principles, and to give you some first steps to take in your own company to begin to turn your own employees into mini-CEOs.

2

Where CEOFlow Came From (My Story)

Sometimes I've believed as many as six impossible things before breakfast."

~ Lewis Carroll

How did companies like Semco, AES, WL Gore, Patagonia, and Google create freedom-based management cultures and inspire employees to help increase revenue year after year? How do you create a company where everyone is encouraged to contribute to the best of their creativity and ability, so that the company can be more successful than conventional command-and-control management culture?

For years I've been obsessed with self-managing systems and companies and have studied what these companies and others practiced.

In the mid-2000's, I worked at Salesforce.com – now a $1 billion+ software company – where I first applied these practices and my CEOFlow system. I created a self-managing inside sales team that helped Salesforce.com add $100 million in recurring revenue.

When I say my team was "self-managing," I could choose to be at work and spend 95% of my time on "important, non-urgent" activities such as vision, culture, and coaching. Or I could choose to step away from the team and let it run itself.

For example, in 2004 I went on safari in Africa for two weeks (this is before they had cell phone service in the Masai Mara). I returned to find that I had nothing to do to catch up on: no issues needed resolving and that sales had grown despite my absence.

The team's self-managing systems also made it possible for the company to promote me because my sales team wasn't dependent on me anymore. I wasn't trapped by my own success.

When I was promoted from sales into mergers & acquisitions, I never had to look back - the team and processes kept on growing smoothly without me. I even joked that they would start growing faster without me around to bug them! (Which, I have to say, turned out to be true.) How often do your employees and executives get more done when you are out of the office or on vacation, and you stop asking them for reports and updates all the time?

Before Salesforce.com, I was founder and CEO of LeaseExchange.com, a 50-person internet company. I learned the hard way what works in management and what doesn't work.

After raising $5 million in venture capital and working through it for a couple of years, we shut down the business in 2001.

As painful as it was, the experience of those years with LeaseExchange prepared me for success at Salesforce.com.

After Salesforce.com, I spent a year as an EIR (Entrepreneur-In-Residence) at Alloy Ventures, a $1 billion venture capital fund. My job was primarily to figure out what I wanted to do next!

Three months into it, I spent a few weeks reflecting while traveling in Asia. I realized that I didn't want to start another software company, raise venture money, and likely become trapped by my own company for years.

When you start a technology company and raise money from professional investors, you're on a one-way track and there's no going back. You may or may not make money after 3-7 years, but you're definitely stressed most of that time. You have a tremendous amount of pressure and responsibility.

Rather than following the same old beaten career path, what I really desired was to be able to *work on what I want, when I want, with whom I want, from where I want – not in some indeterminate future,* **even while starting and growing a new company.**

At Alloy Ventures, in this same period of reflection, I found my life purpose: to help people - like you - *make money through enjoyment*. I describe it one way as combining the best of capitalism (money, abundance) and Buddhism (happiness). Your work can make you both happier and more money, at the same time. It can be enjoyable, freeing, and profitable today if we choose to make it so!

I finally saw clearly that work is hard because we choose to make it hard. I saw that work doesn't have to be difficult for us to make money and have what we want in life such as freedom, fun and fulfillment. If we have a conscious vision of how we want work to work for us, we can have our cake and eat it too!

I learned the hard way what works in management and what doesn't work.

OK you're probably saying to yourself, "That's easy to say for people starting from scratch, but I already have a business. I have responsibilities. It's not that easy." Yes, even you can redesign your work and business to support your life and goals.

That is why I created CEOFlow specifically for CEOs and leaders – to help you create an energizing, productive work environment for yourself, your employees, and your customers - because if one constituency doesn't have flow, the others won't either.

CEOFlow is the systemization of what the founders of successful "freedom" who built self-managing systems and teams, intuitively created.

If they can do it, why can't you?

"Things are only impossible until they're not."
~ Jean-Luc Picard, Star Trek: The Next Generation

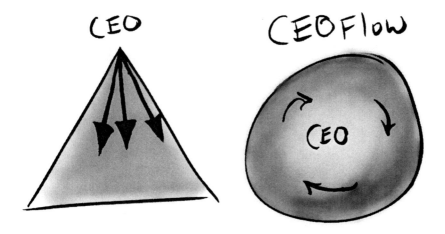

Sketch: CEO Control (Push Management) and CEOFlow (Pull Management)

Conventional management tells us that the CEO needs to set the direction for the company and tell everyone what to do – a top-down model.

This is exhausting for the CEO because you feel like you have the responsibility of the world weighing on your shoulders.

Instead, what if you create an environment where the CEO acts as a hub, while everything flows around them, where the CEO doesn't act as a bottleneck on decisions and responsibilities, but as a catalyst, facilitator, and visionary?

(For the full-color version of this and more sketches, go to www.CEOFlow.com/sketches)

3

Push Management And Pull Management

"Employees will give to the company only as much as they feel they're getting. Want employees to go the extra mile? Start by going the extra mile for them."

~ Aaron Ross

"To lead the people, walk behind them."

~ Lao-Tzu

Are you or your employees working harder, under more pressure, but running in place? The Internet has changed business in helpful and challenging ways:

- We have more information and metrics and more confusion from all the clutter.

- We can develop and deploy products faster far beyond our clients' ability to absorb them.

- We can find prospects more easily but they're less interested in talking with us.

- We have more forecasting tools but less predictability.

- We work harder but not as hard as the scrappy firms in India and China.

I've worked with, mentored, and observed dozens of companies over the past couple of years. It's not uncommon for the double whammy of clutter and pressure to make companies and people so busy that they can't get anything done as busy-ness replaces productivity.

The brute force methods that used to work so well, such as "work harder," "hire more," "spend more" aren't true sustainable or competitive advantages. There will always be other companies that can work harder, hire more people and raise more money

It's time to start taking regular breaths to reflect on what we're missing...

It's time to start taking regular breaths to reflect on what we're missing - better, more creative ways to increase growth more productively.

From the CEOFlow point of view, the most impactful thing a CEO can do to increase sustainable growth is to move towards a Pull Management system and away from a Push Management system. This will help align and engage the creativity and inspiration of everyone, your group mind, rather than just a few select individuals.

How can a CEO create an environment that helps the company to grow itself faster by unlocking the motivation of its people in an environment of trust, transparency, and alignment?

Can a CEO spend 95%+ of their time enjoyably surfing the flow of growing a company, rather than feeling sometimes like they're paddling against the waves?

"Push Management" Is The "Give A Man A Fish" Model

Push Management is the term I use to describe the classic command-and-control style of management, in which the executives tell employees what to do and how to do it. You don't ask for, or want, much feedback from people – you just want them to do the damn job and not complain about it.

Push Management is easier in many ways in the short-term than Pull Management, because you get to just tell people what to do. That doesn't mean they'll do it or do it the way you want...

However, Push Management isn't enjoyable for anyone – either the managers pushing or the employees being pushed. I know no one enjoyed it, including myself, when I practiced it at LeaseExchange.

"Pull Management" Is The "Teach A Man To Fish" Model

Pull Management is the term I use to describe a company culture of focused collaboration and open communication, in which you are dedicated to the success of your company by being first dedicated to the success of your employees.

Pull management takes more patience and commitment, because you aren't allowed to tell people what to do – you have to let them figure it out for themselves, with coaching and guidance, of course.

Rather than trying to control everything, which is an illusion anyway, you focus on creating an environment where people are "pulled" into action by the vision of what is possible and by the opportunity for them to make a difference.

Personal Examples

I've managed at both ends of the spectrum and have seen the night-and-day difference

1) **"Push Management"**: LeaseExchange was a company I cofounded in 1999, which did the "dot-com to dot-bomb" circle. We raised $5 million in venture capital, launched, hired about 40 people, and then went out of business a couple of years later, in 2001.

I was a first-time CEO and manager, and while I did some things very well, I made lots of management mistakes, such as trying to rush-rush-rush everything all the time, not letting people do things their way, second guessing their decisions, and more – I could go on! A lot of what I did was classic Push management, attempting to control things and people.

2) **"Pull Management"**: Salesforce.com. Learning from my mistakes at LeaseExchange, prepared me to succeed at Salesforce.com. I created a inside sales team that sourced $100 million in recurring revenue for Salesforce.com in its first few years. Growth, month after month, year after year, regardless of the people in the team, just kept coming effortlessly because of the team's self-managing, sustainable systems and management culture.

The team culture and organizational system was designed to be as self-managing and sustainable as possible, by creating a Pull environment of trust, transparency, and alignment.

One of the things I am proud of is that the team never missed a beat when I moved to the acquisitions and investments team of Salesforce.com.

There Is No "Right Way" or "Wrong Way"

I understand how easy and tempting it is to make Push "wrong" and Pull "right." And to think of companies as either Push OR Pull. That's not the case; there is always a spectrum.

It's really about finding the balance for your own style between the two that gets you the most results with the most enjoyment of the journey along the way.

Using Both Push And Pull

Even most Pull Management companies will want to switch into Push mode once in awhile when an urgent crisis strikes (such as a fundraising round that falls through) and you don't have the time you need for Pull Management.

Or perhaps in some daily situations people will need to use a little Push energy to get their team or an employee over some kind of hump. When very fast action is needed, a temporary Push Management burst can help get you through a situation.

Just be aware of falling into ongoing Push Management habits that are hard to get rid of once the crisis or situation is dealt with. "I will only do this one time" is a slippery slope. It's easy to keep making decisions for people. It's easy to keep telling them what to do rather than helping them find the answer themselves.

As an analogy, if you're the healthy eater that can have a dessert once in awhile without binging or reverting to bad habits, a single dessert won't make you unhealthy.

If you're the type of healthy eater who falls off the wagon when they have a cookie or a piece of chocolate cake, then you have to be much more vigilant of succumbing to your temptations to use Push Management.

Comparing Push And Pull Management

Companies aren't 100% Pull **or** 100% Push; think of the two as ends of a spectrum in which your company falls somewhere in the middle, such as 80% Push, 20% Pull.

(We have a CEOFlow Push/Pull Survey – see www.CEOFlow.com)

Push Management Culture	Pull Management Culture
The CEO has to keep motivating (pushing) people.	Employees are self-motivated and inspired to work.
Work is tiring and draining.	Work is energizing & enjoyable.
Even the CEO often doesn't look forward to their work.	People look forward to their work or workplace.
The executive team and board come up with the vision and goals and push these out to the company.	The company and executives are highly transparent.
Everyone except the CEO gets the blame for missing goals.	The company culture is enjoyable, nurturing, and collaborative.
Secrecy and confidentiality are more important than transparency.	The company trusts employees to pull what they need from management (advice, information, help) as necessary.
There are regular executive-only offsites and outcomes/insights from them aren't shared transparently with the employees.	Employees inspired to go above and beyond the call of duty.
	All employees have the option to engage in shaping company goals and priorities.
The executive team pushes the employees to hit goals – even when they are highly unrealistic.	Constant clarity and alignment across the company.
Employees only feel motivated to do the minimum for their jobs.	Employees have transparent access to updates on the company's goals and progress towards goals.
The company doesn't trust employees, who must be monitored and pushed to do more.	Very low turnover (for your particular industry).
The company culture high pressure and internally competitive.	Mistakes aren't punished; they are used as coaching and learning opportunities.
Mistakes are punished.	Little burnout – employees have discretion in how and when they can take time off.
Burnout is common or endemic.	Time is built into the company and employees' calendars for reflection on activities, goals and priorities
Turnover is average or above average.	

Example Pull Practices

I held one particularly interesting CEO dinner in Los Angeles in 2008. It was really fun sitting down with a group of like-minded CEOs to discuss how they implement different kinds of Pull Management ideas to help their companies be more self-managing.

Here are some examples of stories that came out in a single event:

Peer-Managed Discretionary Spending:

Sasha Strauss, CEO of Innovation Protocol (brand strategy consulting) has a simple policy: Anyone can spend up to $500 on behalf of the company or a client, no questions asked. They can spend up to $5000 without executive approval if they get approval from any two other team members.

One example of an unintended benefit that would never would have come up if expenses were pre-approved and pre-judged: employees purchased an extra large flat screen TV and an Xbox/Halo gaming system. It turns out clients loved the system and have been known to stay after client meetings to play and bond with employees, strengthening client relationships.

An idea to expand on this: as the company grows, what if Innovation Protocol established a monthly budgeted pool of money for these expenses and then published the spending for all to see?

What if the company used transparency as the self-managing, peer-based feedback mechanism rather than approval processes?

Co-creating With Employees:

To get a project going or completed, you can:

  1) define and assign it, or

  2) co-create it with the people involved.

It's often more convenient, taking less time and energy, and thus tempting to tell people to do things rather than working with them to help them create them together ("co-creation").

Co-creation, involving employees in the creation of the business, takes longer and you have less 'control,' but if you work with someone to co-create the project or goals together (including letting them do it all themselves), they will earn emotional ownership of it, which translates into more inherent motivation.

Alternate Forms Of Rewards:

As another example from Strauss of Innovation Protocol: one time, wanting to specially reward an employee with something other than a pure cash bonus, Strauss offered the employee a $2250 anonymous donation to any charity(s). The employee was incredibly effusive and wrote a multi-page thank you to Strauss!

If you overly depend on cash to reward performance, people will start working just for the money (extrinsic motivation) rather than for the exceptional performance for its own sake and the pleasure of a job well done (inherent motivation).

Different people value different forms of compensation.

Different people value different forms of compensation. What if you gave them, whether as a part of standard compensation plan or a bonus, a choice of cash, equity, more vacation, or an anonymous donation?

Giving employees more control and choice over the aspects and environment of their working world and execution of their job increases motivation.

Publishing Financials:

The CEO of a privately owned company published summary financials of the company to the employees. He was nervous about it the first time, but the employees greatly appreciated it, as it gave them a better picture of how the business fundamentally worked.

This increased their connection to and understanding of the company, both increasing motivation and enabling them to make better business decisions.

A Vacation Honor System:

Strauss' vacation policy is to treat employees as responsible adults: "take it when you need it, no questions asked." Employees don't drop the baton on their responsibilities. They work with their peers to ensure that they aren't leaving at a critical time and that others can cover for them.

Social pressure acts as the feedback mechanism: if someone abused the vacation privileges, word would get around and damage their internal reputation. And, of course, the CEO would notice.

With this system: employees trust the company more and are more energized...

Although originally there was nervousness about the policy, the value of the honor system has been proven as employees are consistently more refreshed and energized.

With this system: employees trust the company more and are more energized, increasing results, and employees become more aware and practiced in using vacation truly as a recharging tool rather than as an escape.

Let Employees Stumble

Executives are tempted to solve employees' problems especially when something important, like a sale or client proposal, is on the line.

By letting them stumble, *especially when it counts,* employees will get a much faster education and developed sense of independence and self-direction. What's the cost of saving the sale if your employee doesn't get the learning of truly being on the line for it, and remains dependent on you on others?

One CEO: "By letting my employees stumble, I rediscovered my weekends and they've ended up surpassing me in what I was teaching them in."

When Do You Come Down Hard On Employees?

A CEO asked me, "this touchy-feely stuff about employees is great, but do you ever drop the hammer?" (That is, get harsh with employees.) Of course! Setting clear boundaries and expectations help create a productive, enjoyable culture. Anarchy isn't fun.

The BEST thing you can do to enliven your culture is help employees who aren't a fit to move on from the company. Negative employees are like rocks in a river – they slow down and disturb the flow. No matter how difficult it is to clear the rocks from your river, your business and quality people will thank you for it and helping the work flow so much more smoothly!

As a last example of the difference in how you treat employees with Push versus Pull Management approaches, consider the enormous difference between assigning goals to someone (Push) and working together to set goals (Pull). Assigning goals without much input saves you time in the short-term, but at the sacrifice of some of your employees' ongoing enthusiasm and creativity.

Sketch: "Customer Love" Essential To Amazing Success

What do $1 billion+ mega-successes like Google, Facebook, Zappos and Salesforce.com have in common?

Their customers LOVE them. Well, in Facebook's case perhaps it's more of co-dependent addictive love...but still, customers love the service and tell their friends about it. Word of mouth is the ultimate form of marketing, and the Internet makes it easy to spread like wildfire – whether it's good or bad.

What example are you setting for your people? Are you trusting and loving them in a way that will in turn encourage them to share it with each other and customers?

Or are you creating fear and stress in your people, which will likewise spill out from them into the market for customers and the market for talent?

(For the full-color version of this and more sketches, go to www.CEOFlow.com/sketches)

4

How I Built A Self-Managing Team At Salesforce.com

"Remember the difference between a boss and a leader; a boss says, 'Go!' – a leader says, 'Let's go!'"

~ E.M. Kelly

If you haven't heard of Salesforce.com, Marc Benioff founded it in 1999. By 2008 Salesforce.com reached more than a billion dollars in annual revenue. Salesforce.com is a software company that sells internet-based services (software-as-a-service) that help companies manage their sales and marketing functions. They are known as THE main leader and innovator in the business-to-business software space. There are two CEO-Flow lessons in my salesforce.com story.

- First: how Salesforce.com treated me as a mini-CEO and empowered me to create a new kind of rockstar sales team that increased their new business growth in the F2000 market by more than 50%.

- Second: how I in turn designed my sales team to be self-managing with its own version of mini-CEOs. In fact, seven years later the team is still using essentially the same sales, management and people processes that made it so successful in its first few years!

41

My Salesforce.com Story That Almost Didn't Happen

Back in 2001, I shut down my company LeaseExchange and took about a year to do consulting and non-work adventures such as an Ironman Triathlon and a 28-day survival course at the Boulder Outdoor Survival School (called the "bug-eating trip" by my friends and family).

By mid-2002 I was ready to commit to a single long-term work opportunity. I knew that before I started another company, I had to know inside and out how to build a phenomenal sales organization. I knew this because my lack of sales knowledge was a major reason - among others - that LeaseExchange failed.

I checked my ego at the door and took the most junior sales role at Salesforce.com...

While raising venture capital and recruiting are forms of selling, and I did have sales jobs in college, I didn't have any technology sales experience. I hadn't sold in the business-to-business world.

I checked my ego at the door and took the most junior sales role at Salesforce.com, paying a total of around $50,000 per year. In case you think I was taking a low salary because I got a lot of stock - I didn't. My offer included only 2,500 options – out of more than 120,000,000 total shares. In dollar terms, if Salesforce.com went public and was valued at $1 billion dollars, my share would be worth less than $25,000.

So I'm not kidding when I say I checked my ego at the door. I went from being CEO of my own company to answering the 800 number sales line at Salesforce.com.

(In fact, if you registered on Salesforce.com's website in late 2002, it's likely I was the person that called and emailed you to find out if you were a possible lead.)

I took the job because I believe that strongly that I, before starting another company, needed an MBA in building world-class sales organizations. I was investing in my future.

I knew that once I was in the door at Salesforce.com, I'd figure things out and carve my own path, and I did. I created an entirely new sales process and inside sales team that helped Salesforce.com add $100 million in incremental recurring revenue over just a few short years, a team that is still going strong seven years later.

The $100 Million Sales Process And Team

In 2003, Salesforce.com had a problem: it had hired a bunch of high-priced field salespeople to bring in and close new business, but they were starving for pipeline and leads. Their rolodexes turned out to be, with very few exceptions, irrelevant.

Salesforce.com's marketing and PR wasn't generating enough leads at large companies to feed the new hires. These expensive salespeople needed leads.

Except for knocking on doors when I had a painting business in college, I'd never done sales or lead generation before joining Salesforce.com. But I knew I could figure out a way to feed them those leads. I didn't know how much I didn't know!

Knowing nothing about lead generation and sales helped me because I brought a fresh perspective to selling. After trying a few cold calls, I realized what a waste of time that kind of work was and immediately gave it up.

I also read a bunch of sales books and then threw them away. Most just say the same things, in different ways, and weren't helpful at all.

I felt like I had to start from scratch.

I ended up creating a sales prospecting process and inside sales team that consistently generated new qualified sales opportunities for the quota-carrying salespeople.

The team I created focused on ONLY ONE thing: generating new qualified sales opportunities from cold companies (ones at which we had no activity or interest) and passing these qualified opportunities to quota-carrying salespeople to close.

> The team I created focused on ONLY ONE thing: generating new qualified sales opportunities

This was all truly incremental revenue. The team only contacted cold new business accounts at which we didn't have a relationship or current interest. The team didn't receive any inbound leads generated by word-of-mouth or marketing.

This sales lead generation process involved no cold calling, which I regarded as a waste of time after experimenting with making cold calls myself.

(It's hard to be in flow or enjoy your work if your sales are stagnant., and as part of CEOFlow I still consult to help companies implement this unique sales process to create predictable revenue.)

In addition to hiring great people, there were three components to the team's system of year-after-year success:

1. Predictable Success and ROI: I created a simple sales prospecting process that was highly effective and highly repeatable and predictable.

a. I designed the process to make it easy for sales reps to succeed, and 95% of them beat their numbers while ramping in their first three months.

b. After about 18 months of results and data, I could predict the future results of new hires on my team. knew that if I hired someone costing $100,000 per year), they would generate per year as much as $3,000,000 in total revenue (subscriptions worth $1,000,000 per year over three years).

2. Self-Managing Systems: Everything was a system, and I designed the team to be self-managing so that it could grow and succeed even when I couldn't spend much one-on-one time with each person. I didn't want to be the bottleneck to the success of the team or of any individual on the team.

3. Sustainability: I designed the team to succeed over the long-term, independently of who was managing it, so that even when I left the team (or if I was hit by a bus) it would continue growing.

You Don't Need A Big Brand Or Money To Get Creative

You don't need a lot of money to create the results, company or life you want. Lack of money is a common excuse for not being creative.

CEOs, entrepreneurs and your employees make all kinds of excuses about why they aren't moving forward with a new idea, business or project: you need more time, more marketing money, your people aren't motivated, you need funding, etc.

None of these are real obstacles to moving forward to get what you want, whether it's higher and more predictable sales or turning your employees into mini-CEOs. You don't need a lot of marketing money in order to ramp up sales.

In case you're thinking, "Easy for you to say - results came easy for you. You were a part of Salesforce.com. Your company was famous. You had a ton of marketing money to spend. You had all kinds of support. What if I want to increase sales but don't have a big brand or big budget?"

Salesforce.com had tried to create this kind of program a couple of times before, and it failed both times, they were done investing in the area for the foreseeable future.

My manager at the time, Shelly Davenport, and I had an interesting design challenge: to create a new business sales process that would succeed without any money or marketing support and at a company that was pretty much unknown in the Fortune 2000 market we were growing into at the time

When we began the effort to build this function in early 2003, very few large companies outside of California had heard of Salesforce.com. 9 out of the 10 times we called a prospect, they asked something along the lines of, "Do you do outsourced sales for customers? Or sales recruiting?"

This was also just after the dot-com bust, and trust of anything ".com" was at an all-time low.

Also, software-as-a-service was NOT yet accepted by large companies as a viable option. Gartner, a famous technology research firm, was still writing big reports about how Salesforce.com was a great fit for small businesses but not for larger companies.

While Salesforce.com spent millions on general marketing, most of it only reached small business decision makers.

I didn't get a budget for my project beyond my own compensation. In fact, looking back, if I had had a big budget or a bunch of people to tell what to do, I wouldn't have been forced to get so creative in solving the problem of how to predictably generate new pipeline for the sales organization

What I did have:

- A phone, a desk, a chair, and a computer (yes, I began by making cold calls, and quickly realized how ineffective they are).

- The Salesforce.com application and an online source for lists of prospects called OneSource (very similar to Hoovers).

- Freedom to experiment for *three months* as a mini-CEO.
- An attitude that this was an interesting design challenge and that it could be fun!
- Commitment to create something meaningful (in terms of sales) to Salesforce.com.
- Belief in myself – moxie!

The point here is that when you're low on resources, by having a clear objective and looking at it as an interesting challenge, you can force yourself (and your employees) to get CREATIVE.

Constraints can lead to more creativity for both yourself and your people.

An Extra Challenge – My CEO, Marc Benioff

To develop mini-CEOs, you will have to let go of your own assumptions, including the ones you "know" are true. Your assumptions often will only stunt your mini-CEOs.

You see, for the first two years of my sales team's existence, Marc Benioff wasn't a believer. He had good reasons. From his experience, these kinds of inside sales teams don't add true incremental value. Either they end up pushing papers for field salespeople who take advantage of the support, or the inside sales reps on the team take credit for leads that they didn't really produce on their own. The tremendous pressure on them to produce increases the likelihood they will try to cheat the system.

It's hard to measure the true ROI of these teams, because of the challenge of measuring their true incremental contribution. A major part of the success of our team at Salesforce.com stemmed from our design of a bulletproof (yet simple) audit process that ensured the integrity of the results the team took credit for. Marc and the executives could trust that all of our results were truly incremental.

Thank you, Marc, for giving us the room to create and prove it out!

I want to acknowledge Shelly Davenport and Frank Van Veenendaal for letting me run with this idea and team as a mini-CEO. They gave me the months of time, political room, support and trust to see if I could make this work.

Part of turning your employees into mini-CEOs includes letting go of your own assumptions. What you know to be true might not be true! Encourage your people to challenge you and experiment, as long as you all have a shared, aligned vision for the company.

How much time and political room do you give your mini-CEOs to make new ventures work? Or does your impatience or assumptions choke off new ideas and breakthroughs before they have a chance to blossom?

It was easier for me to understand and create something that perfectly aligned with what Benioff and Salesforce.com needed because I knew all of the companies goals and priorities through our V2MOM process (Salesforce.com's annual goals planning and alignment process, which I'll describe in the next section).

And because Benioff knew the company had gone through the annual V2MOM alignment processes, he could more easily trust that more people would be able to operate as mini-CEOs.

By the way, Salesforce.com is more of a traditionly-run Push Management, company than a Pull Management company. However, I'm focusing here on sharing what kinds of Pull methods worked there. Even at a Push Management company, you can still successfully practice Pull Management; it is just be more challenging.

Creating And Maintaining Alignment

Alignment is one of the three core CEOFlow values that create conditions in which mini-CEOs can develop (along with Trust and Transparency).

Alignment means you and your people have co-created a common vision, have shared goals, and are working in harmony towards them.

It's one thing to create that alignment in a day, but it's another to maintain it over time. The challenges in maintaining alignment will more likely trip you up than creating it in the first place. Anyone who has a business partner or marriage will know exactly what I mean!

Creating a self-managing sales team at Salesforce.com took constant creation and maintenance of alignment. One thing that made it easier was Salesforce.com's V2MOM process.

Alignment Through Salesforce.com's V2MOM Planning Process

One of Benioff's key business practices that helped Salesforce.com grow to more than $1 billion in revenue in less than 10 years is the V2MOM planning process.

Benioff came up with a plan to set the company's vision and align all of its people and teams in the execution of the vision. The plan stands for Vision, Values, Methods, Obstacles, and Metrics.

It helps the company (and the teams and people in it) lay out a vision, prioritize the most effective methods to achieve that vision, anticipate problems ahead of time, and understand how they will measure success.

This is done at every level in the company. The company as a whole (a Salesforce.com V2MOM), teams (a Corporate Sales V2MOM), and each individual do them (a personal Aaron Ross V2MOM) and even for projects.

This creates alignment up and down the organization, from Benioff down to individual salespeople.

Benioff took the V2VMOM process very seriously. The executive team alone spent 40-100 hours per year just in creating it at the corporate level. It took us about 10-15 hours as a group to create the team version and then about 2-4 hours per individual for their personal versions. It is well worth the investment.

1. **VISION** – what is the big picture? What is your vision for the next 12 months?

- *Example from Corporate V2MOM:* "Double our enthusiastic and wildly successful global customer & partner community through flawless execution of our proven model."

- *Example from my sales team V2MOM:* "Make a difference in the success of our team & company by being the best in the world at generating new business, through constant innovation and the sharing of our expertise."

- *Example from my personal V2MOM:* "Manage team members as a leader who will be remembered 10 years from now as their best ever."

2. VALUES – What are the top 3-4 business values that are most important to keep while working towards that vision? These were usually broad values-based business priorities rather than pure cultural values.

- *Example from Corporate V2MOM:* "Customer Trust" was a top Value during a year that Salesforce.com had recurring uptime and technology problems that were damaging trust with customers and partners. Two other examples include "Flawless Execution" and "Customer Success."

- *Example from my sales team V2MOM:* "Persistency. Efficiency. Success." Each can have multiple meanings. "Success" meant success of each individual on my team, of the sales team, of our prospects and customers, and anyone we came in contact with inside and outside of the company.

- *Example from my personal V2MOM:* "Hands-on Leadership. Watertight Execution. Practical Innovation."

3. METHODS – How will it happen?

- *Example from Corporate V2MOM:* "Increase adoption through sales, service, and partner effectiveness." The V2MOM also goes on to include more detailed specifics about programs and practices to clarify what this actually means.

- *Example from my sales team V2MOM:* "Don't take NO until you get to the VP Sales." While it might seem obvious to have this as a sales method, I found that new salespeople gave up too easily when they received "No" from someone like the VP Marketing. This became a V2MOM method because it was so important to reinforce this practice of never giving up at an ideal prospect until a salesperson connected with a decision maker – for us, the VP Sales.

- *Example from my personal V2MOM:* "Lead from the trenches." I would never ask people to do something I wouldn't or hadn't done. I kept as close to them as possible and involved them in my own world as much as I could.

- *2nd personal example:* "A successful team is made up of successful individuals." By focusing on making every individual successful, the team succeeded.

4. OBSTACLES – What is or could be in the way? What landmines can we proactively plan for or avoid?

- *Example from Corporate V2MOM:* "IT and corporate fear of having data outside the firewall."

- *Example from my sales team V2MOM:* "Easier to work harder than smarter." I view putting in longer and longer hours as a crutch for people who don't know how to redesign their work or process to make it easier to get results. In our culture, it's easy to backslide into two habits to solve problems: "throw hours at it" and "throw money at it".

- *Example from my personal V2MOM:* "Size of team heading to 17 direct reports." The number of my direct reports was a challenge. When a team is growing, people need more attention and coaching. I found it very difficult to give each person individual coaching and attention they needed once the team grew past 10 people. It was this kind of growth that kept me pushing the boundaries of creating self-managing systems, to find ways for peers to help and coach each other.

5. METRICS – How will you measure progress and success?

- *Example from Corporate V2MOM:* Revenue, adoption rates, etc.

- *Example from my sales team V2MOM:* I never measured daily dials or calls. My metrics focused more on a series of results-based metrics such as Conversations Per Day, Qualified Opportunities Per Month, New Pipeline Per Month, and Total Closed Bookings.

- *Example from my personal V2MOM:* I had some key life and Salesforce.com-related career goals here, such as "Make $170,000+ per year next year", "Gain Asia & EMEA operating experience," and "Complete Hawaii Half-Ironman in June 2005."

Reflection: Ryan Martin On The Value Of Creating With (Not For) Your People

Ryan Martin is the Director of Salesforce.com's North American New Business team (the sales team I started). He took over the team from me in 2005, when I moved to a new acquisitions and investments team in Salesforce.com. Ryan has led the team since then while growing it to almost 100 people and more than a half-dozen managers.

Here is how he describes what it was like when we created the culture and team as a group, rather than having me create a vision or systems and push them down onto people:

"I've always been impressed by Aaron's leadership style and have worked hard to incorporate what I learned from him into my own personal style.

One example that comes to mind is when he was thinking through a redesign of the sales stages, and how they were tracked in the salesforce.com application, of the sales process that he created.

He understood that it was important to have the help create and update the process in order for us to adopt it. Rather than creating it on his own and rolling it out, he took a collaborative approach by discussing the purpose of the process, what needed to be accomplished, and then spent parts of team meetings gleaning ideas and feedback from the team in order to refine, get buy-in, and ultimately create a better process.

He and the team recreated it together. Everyone felt ownership of it and thus used it.

Aaron gets the 'group think' concept, removes his ego from the equation, and empowers his people to build something inspiring that's more than the sum of its parts.

He also took this same approach to creating the V2MOM for the team. It was amazing to see how motivated and productive everyone was after being so engrained in the process through Aaron's insight and guidance…and after 5 years (and hundreds of millions of dollars later), it's clear that the cultural DNA he injected works like a charm!"

How To Get Started Designing Self-Managing Teams And Processes

Ready to starting shifting your teams towards more self-management? Let's assume you have gone through at least the "Vision" portion of V2MOM or your own planning process, and you and your the team has created a vision that includes a full or partial vision of turning your employees into mini-CEOs.

The employees buy in because they want more control over their work and desire to become self-managing – even to the level of the janitor picking their own hours to come in and clean.

I recommend doing the following process with a single team first, such as a sales team, to find out what works for your culture before moving on to other teams. Patiently and persistently keep at shifting the culture and teams towards the common vision. Be prepared for it to take longer than you think, because you are dealing with changing habits and habits don't like to change

Start by asking these two questions:

1. How would the team operate if the manager disappeared tomorrow?

2. What would have to happen for the team to not just continue operating as its current level, but to actually improve its results?

For example, here are some common key responsibilities of a VP Sales:

- Goal setting and achievement

- Personal involvement in big deals

- Culture

- Compensation – designing, calculating, reporting

- Talent – structuring roles, hiring, firing

- Coaching

- Analysis and reporting

- Budgeting / expenditures

- Process design and improvement

Take your list and start at the top and brainstorm your way down, point by point. For example, how would "Goal Setting and Achievement" work if the VP Sales disappeared tomorrow and wasn't replaced?

If you get stuck or feel like you want to cheat and pretend only one person can be the owner of that point, remember what Charles de Gualle said: "The graveyards are full of indispensable men."

As you finish going through the list, a vision will shape as to how the team can self-manage itself. Don't try to implement every point on your list at once. Select a few (two or three) of the points that are the most important and easiest to implement, before moving on to the other points. Build some momentum with initial successes.

What's In It For The VP Sales (Or Any Manager)?

If you start giving away all the responsibilities and power of a manager, won't they feel threatened that you won't need them? No!

The more a sales team can manage itself, the more the VP Sales can focus on developing the "important, not urgent" aspects of the team, such as talent, culture and vision, rather than fighting fires or spending time on daily, "unimportant but urgent" tasks.

Even better, by freeing up their own time and energy, the VP Sales (and other executives) can take on more of your (the CEO's) responsibilities, and this allows you freedom and energy for even bigger things yourself!

See how this works? You get what you give. Create more freedom and upside for your people, and you'll get it in turn

When Distributing Responsibilities, Begin With Elimination

As you work through your list of responsibilities and tasks, it's a perfect opportunity to use the 80/20 rule to clear out non-essential tasks. Rather than distributing 100% of the work of the manager, divide the work into two parts: 1) the 20% that is the most important to keep within the team or company, and 2) the 80% that can be eliminated, automated, or outsourced.

You can do this with two columns on a whiteboard: "Important 20%" and "Other 80%." In the 80% column, how can you first eliminate as much as possible?

Work through the responsibilities this way:

1. What can you Eliminate?
2. What can be Automated?
3. What can you Outsource?
4. Finally, Delegate or Distribute what is left.

For functions that can't be eliminated, how can you use the core CEOFlow values of Transparency and Trust to eliminate 80% of the reporting, monitoring, checking and auditing? (You can see more examples in the chapter on The Power Of Transparency.)

For example, rather than having a process to pre-approve expenditures, try eliminating the approval process entirely, and transparently publish everyone's expense reports or team expenditures against budgets.

> *...rather than having a process to pre-approve expenditures, try eliminating the approval process entirely...*

In that kind of expenditures system, create a process in which individuals must seek advice from others before spending money. It could be a process in which a peer, not a manager, must approve the expenditure. Peer review and transparency are a much more powerful and productive combination than administrative rules and regulations.

Then after eliminating and reducing as much as possible, go through and map out what you can automate or outsource, in ways that will both free your time and improve results.

After you've created plans for eliminating, automating, and outsourcing as much as possible, move on to delegating.

Distributing Management Through Sub-Teams And Team Leads

I will use a couple of terms here: (1) "Team Lead" and (2) "[*Specific Function*]" Lead, like "Training Program Lead."

When a group grows past 8-10 people, it is easy to begin losing that intimate, small team feel. People start feeling lost in a crowd, or that they can hide.

When my sales team grew to 15 direct reports, well past my ability to give each person the amount of attention they deserved, I divided the team into three sub-teams of 5 people.

Each sub-team then selected their own "team lead", like a squad leader, who would best support them in their personal sales success.

These team leads were not managers but salespeople with extra responsibilities around ensuring their sub-team functioned smoothly. They were my mini-CEOs that took over my daily and, to me, lower-value tasks like compensation reports (which were high-value to them, because they were learning and developing).

While I often didn't have people on my team for more than 8 months (because we were growing so fast, and I kept promoting people), I would recommend you make team lead roles rotating positions, say every three-to-six months, so different people can develop and practice leadership skills.

Creating Sub-Teams Without Single Team Leads

Another way to create self-managing teams is, rather than having any sort of team leads at all, spread responsibilities across the team by creating functional leads: "Goals Setting Lead," "New Hires Lead," "Education Lead," "Coaching System Lead," "Recruiting Lead," etc. You can rotate these roles every few months. Part of the responsibilities of an outgoing Lead is always to train the incoming Lead.

A functional lead doesn't have to be the one doing all the work. They are only responsible for it getting done, whether or not they do it.

A "Research Lead" could be responsible for managing an outsourced firm that is doing the actual research. A "Sales Hiring Lead" could be responsible for organizing the hiring process and making sure the interviews get done, without actually doing any interviews themselves.

A Team Leads Example

When you have a function that does need internal ownership by someone (like coaching of new hires), select a *single* person to be responsible for it — no committees. Make them a mini-CEO of that function.

Whether or not that person does the actual work isn't important. What is important is they are responsible for it getting done and *better than before.*

For example, before I created my team leads & sub-teams system, I spent at least half of my time coaching and training new hires. As the team grew,

I wasn't able to give them and the veteran sales reps the time and attention they all deserved. When we moved to a team leads and sub-teams system, my sales team leads took over 80%+ of the first few weeks of training and coaching for any new hire that entered their own sub-team. Each team lead ensured the new hire ramped up on time over the first 6 weeks. I was free to coach the veterans on even more advanced sales skills.

Everybody won: new hires got more training and attention, veterans got more attention from me, and I could spend my own time on higher value work (such as coaching veterans on their career path instead of teaching new hires how to use Salesforce.com).

The team leads didn't do all of the coaching themselves; they were responsible for ensuring a new hire on their sub-team was trained and coached. After that I would then come in and spend more time with them, when they were ready for more advanced 1-1 coaching.

To align their goals with the goals of their sub-team, 20% of a team lead's goals and compensation depended on the whole sub-team's results. This 20% was extra compensation for taking on the responsibility of being a team lead.

The other 80% of a team lead's compensation depended on their individual sales performance.

Some of the other functions that the sub-teams and team leads owned included:

- Quality control of the work produced (we had an audit process to verify sales results and deals before approving them as commissionable).

- Small incentive/marketing budgets for their sub-team.

- Fun activities for their sub-team.

- Interviewing and training of new hires in their sub-team.

- Peer reviews of each other.

- Monthly achievement of sub-team sales goals.

I focused much of my time on coaching the team leads – training the trainers. As part of that, I still walked around and talked and sat with everyone, including new hires. Staying connected to the trenches gave me more insight into how to better help the team leads and improve our   systems.

How To Distribute Responsibilities

You need to distribute responsibilities throughout the team (or to outside the team), in ways that don't add a lot of extra work, hence the importance of elimination, automation and outsourcing before delegation.

By distributing responsibilities to the employees touching customers, the ones closest to the action, you can get better quality work and results. They will learn much more about the business and what it takes to succeed as mini-CEOs.

Going back to the list of common VP Sales responsibilities, here are some examples taken from the above list of common sales management responsibilities:

Goal Setting:

What conditions would have to exist for the team to be able to set and achieve its own goals better than before?

- 80/20 rule: how much of the goals setting process isn't that important? Do you really need to set and track 15 goals? What are the 20% of the goals that matter the most?
- What if you have a "Goals Setting Lead" on the team to be the point person to manage the process, both within the team and with the CEO?
- Do you need a separate "Quota Beating Lead" to monitor & report on the teams overall progress each month, and flag areas of concern?

Senior Help On Big Deals:

If you have to throw your VP Sales (or yourself) at every big deal, you don't have a scalable sales process, and that one person will always be a bottleneck. In fact, any time a single person is a bottleneck to any process, your growth is capped.

What conditions would have to exist for 80% of your current big deals to close without help from the VP Sales or CEO?

- Can you enhance your sales process or product to reduce the need for VP Sales involvement? To make deals easier to win without as much help?

- Which other senior executives can be placed "on call" to step into big deals?

- Could customers who love you contribute some of their time to helping you? (Yes, this can happen, especially if you have a special privileges program for them.)

Sales Reporting And Analysis:

What conditions would have to exist for the team and executives to get all the reports and analysis they need with the click of a button?

- By publishing the sales results in real-time, such as with an application like Salesforce.com, can you eliminate the need for someone to do reporting altogether?

- Be aware of data-addiction. Which reports are nice-to-have versus need-to-have? It is common for executives and board members who ask for reports to forget that many take considerable time and energy to produce, and that time isn't free because it takes people away from the business. Rather than blindly producing reports, ask them their business goal for the report. Maybe they need something other than what they want. Help executives understand the cost of the reports they want, so they can prioritize their requests.

- How can you redesign your reports to be more useful? Often times reports are created just because someone wants it without a clear idea of its purpose. Ask "What decision will this report help you make better? What is the goal of this report?" If a report doesn't help you prioritize your energies or make better decisions, something's wrong with it.

Culture:

A lot of companies just talk about culture, but do little about it. How much do you do to encourage and develop a positive culture that attracts and supports great people? What conditions would have to exist for the culture to identify and practice its key values?

- Example: if having fun is important to your culture (and it better be!), the team could have a Fun Lead who would be accountable for the team having fun each week. No, "accountable fun" is not an oxymoron. When people are busy, it's easy to forget to have fun.

- Again, that person may or may not be the person organizing events, instigating practical jokes, or starting impromptu office karaoke sessions – they only need to make sure it happens regularly.

An Example Of Engaging The Whole Team In Designing Their Compensation

Even when I retained some core responsibilities – comp plan design, V2MOM / vision planning, annual planning – I still gave everyone the option of getting involved in those functions, if they wanted to. Involving employees (or giving them the option of involvement) in the creation of *everything* is vital to inspiring them to care about the business as much as you do.

For example, at one point several sales team members were expressing frustration about the design of the compensation plan, which had three components:

- A fixed base salary,

- A variable commission based on how many qualified (and audited/confirmed) opportunities that person generated in a month, and

- A variable commission based on how much revenue had been sourced by that person.

The complaints were a little varied but ultimately came down to the fact that I hadn't taken enough time to educate some of the newer sales reps on why we had that system.

Rather than just telling them why it was designed that way, I set up a process to get the team's help to revisit and redesign the comp plan. Out of about 15 people at the time, 5 opted-in to help.

We had one main session to dig into the issue, to review the team's priorities and goals (identified through the V2MOM process), and to create a forum for them to share their ideas on how to better shape the comp plan to support the goals.

After a couple hours of discussion, which included revisiting even the basic assumptions around how we measured performance and success, and if we should use different metrics, the team came to the conclusion that the current comp plan was the best one.

Rather than just telling them why the comp plan evolved into its current form, I led them through their own discovery process. They "got it" and the complaints stopped. Even better, they could be much more effective in teaching other team members or new hires about the comp plan so these frustrations didn't pop up again with the next generation of new team members.

We ended up in the same place we began: the comp plan didn't change. One could feel like we wasted time, but I felt it was a fantastic use of time as a coaching exercise and as a way to increase trust and transparency in the team. The reps felt more connected to the team and the systems because they now more intimately understood where everything came from and why.

My only disappointment was that I hoped they would come up with something that I had missed and that we could improve the plan!

Transparent Compensation And Reporting

I had a convenient advantage that helped me transparently publish everyone's compensation on the team: they all were on the same basic plan structure (same base salary, same bonus and commission rates). No one had special deals even though some people had much more experience than others. Those with more experience or expectations could earn the extra compensation through higher results.

With transparency compensation, the whole team could see who earned the most and why – how their higher results translated directly into more money.

Publishing compensation also eliminated compensation and payroll errors, and reduced by 80% the amount of time I had to spend on tracking and reporting compensation. If you haven't tracked and reported on compensation, it's a pain. For a long time, we used spreadsheets at Salesforce.com to report commissionable results.

The secrecy model:

- Run the reports – what were each person's results?
- Prepare the report and calculate commissions.
- Cut the report into private reports for each person.
- Email or sit with each person to share results and ensure correctness.
- Fix the report as necessary.
- Combine all the results into one spreadsheet.
- Send to finance.

And that is when it works. If there is some issue in the report or with finance, the process gets into a painful circle of "fix-resend-check-fix-resend-check…"

When the team grew past a handful of people, I started using transparency to eliminate 80% of this work and improve the process.

I put all the sales results into a single spreadsheet, with the calculated commissions.

I then emailed the entire sheet to the whole team. Everyone could see everyone's results, and how they ranked.

Yes, everyone could see on our Salesforce.com dashboards how they ranked in numbers of opportunities or deals, but in the spreadsheet they could rank themselves by total compensation.

They could see exactly who was doing the best and thus whom they could model or go to for advice (we had a culture of helping each other succeed).

They could see if there were any problems with the report. They felt confident that they would get the right paycheck from finance, which is not true for many organizations – compensation payment issues are common.

They could trust in the process and not worry about it, because we were open and transparent with it.Ultimately, switching to this transparent process made comp reporting a snap for me and for them!

I never took it to the next level, which would have been to have someone volunteer to be the Comp Lead, to manage the reporting and processing for me. But that would have been an easy next step.

Example Of A Self-Managing Weekly Meeting

Some functions can be designed to be self-managing without a designated leader. My team had a "Salesforce University" meeting every Wednesday afternoon for ongoing education. We modeled it after the Toastmasters public-speaking organization format, and customized it for our specific business needs.

It was self-organizing. Each week someone would volunteer or would be volunteered if they were shy and needed a kick in the pants to manage the next week's agenda and meeting.

The agenda often included a mix of topics in 10-15 minute chunks, such as:

- Product or sales training,

- General business topics (like understanding financial statements or how to manage people),

- Public speaking: sales reps would present to the whole team for practice & feedback,

- "Dealer's Choice" – anything the agenda owner wanted to include just for fun.

The Meeting Leader for that week didn't have to create the content for the next meeting; they were just responsible for finding speakers, organizing them, and running the meeting. This was their own opportunity to begin developing mini-CEO skills at a very basic level.

Here is a specific example of a Salesforce University (SalesforceU) agenda:

- **Meeting Leader Opening (1 min):** Gets meeting started on time. Introduces first speaker. Keeps the meeting on track and on time.

- **Sales Skills 1 (10-20min):** We usually used this block for public speaking/presentation practice, from simple first-time presentations up to a full sales role-play exercise, including a business scenario, pitch, objection handling, and competition. Before moving on, Meeting Leader asks team to share immediate feedback with the speaker.

- **Quick Questions (10-15 min):** A team member prepares 4-5 questions that prospects commonly ask and calls on people to answer them – they get their feet put to the fire! The questions require 1-2 minute answers. Examples: objections, competitive questions, best practice/training questions. After each answer, other teammates quickly share feedback/better answers.

- **Sales Skills 2 (10-20 min):** A second bite-sized session to practice public speaking, role-play phone calls, demos, etc.

- **New Best Practice (10 min):** The topic owner shares one of their own best practices or finds a coworker's worth sharing.

- **Industry/Vertical Learning (15 min):** Each week we select a vertical for someone to research.

  They update the team with information that helps prospect and sell more effectively: terminology, business model fit (or lack thereof), targeted discovery questions, current reference customers, etc. The content owner of this section is the person that learns the most about this topic and becomes the team expert.

- **Meeting Leader Closing (5 min):** Closes the meeting by:

  - Asking for feedback on the SalesforceU format – should it change for next week?
  - Choose a SalesforceU Lead for the next session.
  - Content owners for the next week are determined.

The new SalesforceU Lead writes down the updated roles and is responsible for making following week's meeting successful.

Meetings averaged about 1 hour to 1:30, and the meeting leader was responsible for keeping it on time (another great mini-CEO skills practice). Once in awhile we organized special sessions, such as a full-team demo practice exercise.

The manager's only participation is, along with everyone else in the room, to share feedback with speakers. I had to consciously pull my energy back and resist "managing." The more I put my energy and presence into the meeting, the less space there was for people to share their own energy.

The SalesforceU Lead may not have run a meeting before or might even have been new to Salesforce.com. It is their responsibility to ask for help and advice about how to have a successful result. There was no shortage of expertise all around them, and there was no excuse for not tapping into it. With the meeting-to-meeting handoff of roles, and a feedback mechanism built in, the meeting becomes a self-perpetuating engine.

When Implementing, Be Aggressively Patient

Be aggressive in moving towards this model, of making changes and trying new methods.

Be patient with how much time it will take for people to grow into and run with their new responsibilities. Plan for several weeks or longer - not several days! Keep pushing the boundaries, taking baby steps and practicing patience.

No matter how long it takes, stay committed to your vision of turning your people into mini-CEOs. Just keep taking baby steps and pushing ahead, and practice patience while your people either step into the opportunity or fall out.

Keeping It Fresh

Routines get stale. There is always a need to keep things fresh. As a team we'd regularly reflect on programs like SalesforceU and determine if they were stale and needed refreshing, or whether just putting it on hold for a couple of weeks was enough.

We had two perfect opportunities to do this: both in real-time in the meetings themselves and during V2MOM planning.

Also, how often you schedule things matter. We had new people coming into the team every month, and so weekly worked for us. Doing it every two weeks or once per month might be a better rhythm for your organization. Experiment to see what works.

Better to do it less frequently or have shorter sessions and leave people a little hungry, rather than making too often and thus routine and boring. As with prospects, always leave them wanting a little more!

Supercharge Creativity And Communication With Optional Meetings

How can you make the event more interesting? Here's one way to force yourself and your people to get creative: follow Semco's meeting policy.

Semco has a policy of "every meeting is optional." This forces people to make meetings relevant, useful, and entertaining. Mandatory meetings (which SalesforceU was, I admit) are an easy way to avoid having to get creative in how you serve your people.

I can hear you thinking, "My people are busy, so it's not realistic for me to try to get their attention all the time. If I don't have mandatory meetings, they won't show up."

If you can't even get your own people's attention – the people you pay – how well are you and they going to be able to get your prospects' and markets' attention?

Consider the "meetings are optional policy" as a live-fire, ongoing marketing training experience for everyone in your company.

Plus, if someone holds meetings and no one shows up, they will get instant feedback that

a) What they are doing is not important to others,

b) They aren't communicating effectively why it matters, or

c) Perhaps others just don't like them.

If all your meetings were optional, how would that force you and your people to get focused on what really matters and ensure it is communicated in ways that others (internally or externally) see that?

Why Do Salespeople Resist Following Directions? Maybe You Are Dis-serving Rather Than Serving Them

Executives from every company bemoan how their salespeople (and all other kinds of employees) don't follow processes, programs or directions. If all the programs, tools, and rules that you've created *actually* help salespeople sell more *and* they have been communicated effectively, wouldn't salespeople be adopting more of them? So why don't they?

I'm going to use sales as the specific function and example for how to help employees get things done in a way that you see is beneficial to the company, such as following a sales process, but you can apply the principles anywhere in your organization.

The Push Management model is about telling people what to do – and they do it. Every sales executive and manager gets frustrated with salespeople not doing as they're told: *They don't use the sales force automation system...they don't make enough calls...they don't sell to value...they don't understand their compensation plan...our training session attendance is poor...they don't forecast....*

One option is to bang your head against the wall as much as you want to, trying to force or coerce salespeople into doing things. However, it's a very painful and frustrating way to try to drive behavior. This is Push Sales Management.

And it doesn't even work very well anymore with these uppity, demanding employees we have now who don't want to be ordered what to do and how to do it!

Why:

1) People hate to be told what to do, and thus coercion actually creates resistance.

How do you feel when someone tells you to do something? Do you want to comply, or do you purposely want to not do it just to show them they can't tell you what to do?

2) It's a quick fix, not a solution.

Coercion is an attempt to find a shortcut around better user design. Great design is hard and takes time, and with our "urgency addicted" culture, we tend to think "How can we get this done now? How can we roll this out now?" Especially in sales, where there's always pressure for immediate results!

3) You're going to lose the complexity battle.

All the sales programs, tools, plans, and rules only seem to get more complicated and grow over time. At some point, the complexity crosses an inflection point from "useful" to "hairball."

It's challenging balancing the values of more features and usability.

The best way to fight this battle is to improve the design of the product (your internal processes, tools. and programs) with regular feedback and help from your users (your salespeople).

This doesn't work unless you take the listening seriously. If you give lip service to listening and adopting feedback, nothing will change. Worse, should you ask for input and not institute any of it, you risk leaving your staff feeling undervalued which leads to morale issues, lowered productivity, and stressed staff.

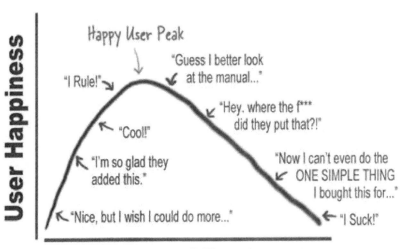

The Featuritis Curve

Happy User Peak

"I Rule!"

"Guess I better look at the manual..."

"Cool!"

"Hey. where the f*** did they put that?!"

"I'm so glad they added this."

"Now I can't even do the ONE SIMPLE THING I bought this for..."

"Nice, but I wish I could do more..."

"I Suck!"

User Happiness

Number of Features

Source: the "Creating Passionate Users" blog

Your people aren't lazy, stubborn, or process-averse. *They are just averse to complicated processes that don't make sense to them, weren't explained properly, or don't help them.* In fact, they love intuitive processes and tools that help them sell more.

So, this thing you want salespeople to do, is it something that will truly help them, or is it more of an administration function for your own benefit? The latter is okay, but you need to explain *why* it is important to the salespeople before they will buy in. Use the word "because" a lot in your communications.

Salespeople are all very busy, with all kinds of demands competing for their attention, so they instinctively prioritize their time.

Unless the tool or idea given to them is intuitive, they'll dismiss spending the mental time and energy to figure it out, and aren't most of us the same way?

Use Pull Management To Better Serve Your People

Here is how you can begin using Pull Management to help your salespeople become more successful by increasing program and process adoption through better design.

First, start learning how to earn, rather than demand, their attention. (Optional meetings, anyone?)

Instead of trying to push mandates or arbitrary programs onto salespeople, try a different approach: consider how you market to customers.

You earn the business and attention of customers. What if you tried thinking of salespeople as customers or users, and your tools, sales environment, and programs are the "products"?

Can you force your customers to do things? No. You have to design a product or service that they appreciate and that improves their business. And in doing so, you earn the business and attention of your customers. The same can be done for your internal customer - your salespeople.

What if you tried thinking of salespeople as customers or users

By the way, if you're having customer and marketing problems, part of it could be a reflection of what's not working with your internal marketing and servicing of your own employees.

Consider what could happen if you made your sales organization 'salesperson-centric'? And since they're the ones actually working with customers and selling stuff, that can only be a good thing. You're also showing them by example how to be customer- and employee-centric themselves as mini-CEOs.

If you focused on usability and return on salespersons' invested time, how would you redesign your sales environment, organization, and tools?

One way to consider where the bar is to consider this: whatever you want salespeople to spend time on should be at least as valuable to them as calling a prospect or customer.

You want to involve the sales teams in the identification, selection and design of initiatives, so they can feel like they are owners and get their input in early and become champions once it's ready to roll-out.

Three Ways To Inspire And Improve The Sales Organization

1) Include salespeople in planning and design of everything

Start by asking the sales organization about how they want to have their voices included in the business. What would they change, what would they do if they managed it?

Just as getting customer insight is important early in the product design process, you can save yourself a lot of frustration and get a much better 'sales product' by including salespeople early in the design process.

You don't have to mandate feedback or ideas, just ask for volunteers (people don't necessarily want to contribute, but they do want to choice to be able to contribute).

There will be a reasonable number of people who want to actively help, either by offering ideas or in actually driving the process, so try letting them.

2) Beta test new programs

Draft your program or rule, and then submit it to groups for feedback. Beta test it. Catch bugs or design issues early, before it's released to everyone.

Yes, this means you'll need to plan next years' territories and comp plans BEFORE the end of this year (shocking, I know!)

3) Survey satisfaction

How satisfied are your salespeople with the support they get and their environment? What tools or parts of the environment most need to be changed?

You can do this by walking the halls, posing the question in sales meetings, or using a simple service like www.surveymonkey.com.

It takes more work, but involving the sales force in the design of its own products will raise morale and engagement and improve their sales tools, both of which lead to more results.

Try this out with your sales organization, and then move to practicing it across the company.

It's great mini-CEO development: by leading by example, you will be showing your people how to better serve each other and their customers.

5

An Introduction To The Concept of "Flow"

"Flow is the mental state of operation in which the person is fully immersed in what he or she is doing by a feeling of energized focus, full involvement, and success in the process of the activity."

~ Mihaly Csíkszentmihályi

Mihaly Csíkszentmihályi is the widely recognized guru of "flow" and the author of *Flow: The Psychology of Optimal Experience.*

What if the CEO and all the employees could work in that state of "energized focus, full involvement and success in the process of the activity"? How powerful would that company be?

If you only remember one thing about flow, remember a key principle of when flow can occur:

Flow happens when work is challenging but not too challenging.

When something is too easy, it isn't fun – it's boring. When something is too hard, it isn't fun either – it's stressful.

The trick is to make your own and your employees' work challenging enough to be interesting but not so challenging as to be discouraging.

Below are some more details from Mihaly on the specific conditions that help lead to flow and how to identify the feeling.

71

Flow for Individuals

Mihaly describes what it feels like for a single person to be in flow:

- *Completely involved, focused, concentrated* – a consequence of innate curiosity or the result of training.
- *Sense of ecstasy* – of being outside everyday reality.
- *Great inner clarity* – knowing what needs to be done and how well it is going.
- *Knowing the activity is doable* – that the skills are adequate, and neither anxious nor bored.
- *Sense of serenity* – no worries about self, feeling of growing beyond the boundaries of ego – afterwards feeling of transcending ego in ways not thought possible.
- *Timeliness* – thoroughly focused on present, don't notice time passing.
- Intrinsic motivation – whatever produces "flow" becomes its own reward.

So how do you get there? Wikipedia says the following conditions help:

- Clear goals (expectations and rules are discernable).
- A high degree of concentration on a limited field of attention (a person engaged in the activity will have the opportunity to focus and to delve deeply into it).
- Direct and immediate feedback (successes and failures in the course of the activity are apparent, so that behavior can be adjusted as needed).
- Balance between ability level and challenge (the activity is neither too easy nor too difficult).
- A sense of personal control over the situation or activity.

The activity is intrinsically rewarding, so there is an effortlessness of action

Achieving Flow In Groups

Mihaly believes that the physical environment for teams makes an enormous difference in getting to flow. At first, the "no-tables" one is a surprise because we are so table-trained, but in the end, it makes a lot of sense.

Some of his suggestions include:

- Creative spatial arrangements: Chairs, pin walls, and charts—no tables! Work is primarily done standing and moving.

- Playground design: Charts for information inputs, flow graphs, project summary, craziness, safe place (people can say what is usually only thought), result wall, and open topics.

- Working with a common vision, goals, and values.

- Prototyping and experimentation.

- Using visualizations to increase productivity.

- Differences between individuals are appreciated as opportunities rather than problems.

Two Examples Of What Gets You Out Of The Flow

1) Politics and favoritism:

A major constraint on people enjoying what they are doing is the conscious fear of how they appear to others and what these others might think.

Any kinds of politics reduce flow for both employees and management.

2) Routines that never change:

When nothing changes and work is routine enough to become boring, flow becomes hard to maintain because the challenge goes away.

Stepping outside of normal daily routines is an essential element of flow. This can be as simple as changing the order of your activities or who is on your team, changing your physical environment, and even changing where you sit. When you change where you sit, you literally see the world from a new perspective!

6

Case Study: Semco

"Even though our workers can veto a deal or close a factory with a show of hands, Semco grows an average of 40 percent per year and has an annual revenue of more than $212 million."

~ Ricardo Semler, *The Seven Day Weekend*

Semco is a multi-hundred-million dollar company based in Sao Paolo, Brazil, with several thousand employees around the world. They have about a dozen different business divisions, most of which manufacture premium industrial products (enormous industrial pumps, for example). They do not operate in commoditized markets.

Semco is more like a group mind, an ant colony. This is quite different from a typical top-down organization that is more analogous to a pack of lions led by a dominant male on the hunt. I realize that lions are sexier than ants, but which type of animal has been more successful on the planet?

Although Semco is an extreme example, their company culture demonstrates the virtues of a company and culture that successfully runs itself through empowerment, inspiration, and trust in its people.

A Warning Label

Do not blindly copy any of Semco's practices here. Semco is an extreme example of CEOFlow. Its practices can be like a loaded gun – effective with good judgment, dangerous when used in ignorance.

Use your judgment on how best to take what Semco has done and make it work in spirit for your own company.

Developing a self-managing culture of mini-CEOs takes vision, commitment and patience. Take baby steps when playing and experimenting with the ideas that Semco has had success with.

A Case Of Extreme CEOFlow And Mini-CEOs

Semco has been my main inspiration for CEOFlow. Ricardo Semler's books about the company gave me many ideas for how to make my sales team at Salesforce.com into a self-managing system. Semco isn't some small-time company with a short-term track record, but when it comes to management practices, it breaks all the rules.

Since Semco switched from a conventional top-down, Push Management style to an employee-driven Pull Management style about two decades ago, it has grown from a few million dollars in revenue to a multi-hundred-million dollar company.

Even more impressive, Semco is based in Brazil and has succeeded despite huge economic swings and chaos.

Part of their success in weathering the economic storms was because of its focus on turning its employees into mini-CEOs, because during stressful times, the employees banded together as a team to help the company continue to survive and thrive.

As I shared at the very beginning of the book, Semco is an example of "Extreme CEOFlow". Here is an introduction to Semco's Way by Ricardo Semler:

> *"Semco has no official structure. It has no organizational chart. There's no business plan or company strategy, no two-year or five-year plan, no goal or mission statement, no long-term budget.*
>
> *The company often does not have a fixed CEO. There are no vice presidents or chief officers for information technology or operations.*
>
> *There are no standards or practices. There's no human resources department. There are no career plans, no job descriptions or employee contracts.*

No one approves reports or expense accounts. Supervision or monitoring of workers is rare indeed.

Strange, eh?

My summary may make Semco sound like a company with an offbeat management style that wouldn't succeed anywhere else. Nevertheless, hundreds of corporate leaders from around the world have visited Sao Paulo to find out what makes us tick.

The visitors are curious about Semco because they want what we have—huge growth in spite of a fluctuating economy, unique market niches, rising profits, highly motivated employees, low turnover, diverse products, and service areas.

Our visitors want to understand how Semco has increased its annual revenue between 1994 and 2003 from $35 million a year to $212 million when I - the company's largest shareholder – rarely attend meetings and almost never make decisions.

They want to know how my employees, with a show of hands, can veto new product ideas or scrap whole business ventures."

Semco was founded in the 1950s as a company manufacturing centrifuges for the vegetable oils industry. Over the years, Semco has leveraged the ideas of its people to expand successfully into the environmental consultancy area, facilities management, real estate consultancy, inventory services and mobile maintenance services, industrial equipment area, and solutions for postal and document management.

> At Semco, people work with substantial freedom, without formalities and with a lot of respect.

At Semco, people work with substantial freedom, without formalities and with a lot of respect. Everybody is treated equally, from high-ranking executives to the lowest ranked employees. This doesn't mean that everyone is paid the same, but the work of each person is given its true importance and everybody is much happier at work.

Their largest shareholder is Ricardo Semler, the son of the founder. Semler has been the driving force in turning Semco into a freedom organization where people enjoy their work and contribute to the success of the company. Semler has written two books about their company and culture: *Maverick* and *The Seven Day Weekend*, both of which I highly recommend.

Question EVERYTHING (Including Authority)

Semler hates taking the conventional rules of work at face value. His favorite question to ask is *Why?*, even regarding things we take for granted:

- Why does a workweek have five days?
- Why do the same job year after year?
- Why grow your company? Why not shrink it?
- Why nine-to-five?
- Why not design financial reports that everyone in the company can understand?
- Why not admit you screwed up?
- Why bother going to all the trouble of finding out what went wrong?
- Why are job titles important to the customer?
- Why have a permanent CEO?
- Why not make meetings optional?

If there's one cardinal strategy that forms the bedrock of Semco's practices, it's the idea of "never making assumptions by always asking why about everything".

People are conditioned to accept things at face value; they are taught not to question. "Why? Because that's the way we do things here."

If you follow conventional rules, you'll get conventional thinking and get conventional results, which is fine if you want that. It's safe. It's the devil you know. It can be scary or feel risky to change the way you manage.

If you follow conventional rules, you'll get conventional thinking

Yet if you want motivated employees, sustainable success and more personal freedom, if you want to turn your employees into mini-CEOs, you must allow them to think for themselves and challenge rules (both inside your company or your marketplace).

Mini-CEOs always question. They don't take things for granted. They understand "the why", so that they can make their own conclusions on the best way to lead forward.

This is hard for the executives who aren't comfortable with employees challenging them, their ideas or plans – basically, challenging their status or ego. Managers with a "just what I tell you to do" attitude will train employees to not think for themselves and to blindly follow directions. These are not mini-CEOs.

Job Passion

This is my favorite quote about job passion:

> *"It's a disservice to expect everyone to feel passion for their jobs."*
> *- Ricardo Semler.*

As much as I believe in and want people to be passionate about their work, it's not realistic to expect everyone to feel that way. It's also not realistic to expect someone who does love their work to be passionate or inspired about it every day.

There's a continual ebb and flow to work and life, and resisting that can actually make you unhappier. Let go of the guilt of not feeling passionate every day, and just focus on continuing to improve bit by bit.

Here are a variety of examples of business practices at Semco, to give you a taste of how they think, work and how their culture feels.

A Transparent Open Books Policy And Financial Literacy

During some economic crises in Brazil, Semco's employees rallied to support the company with their own cost-saving ideas.

Semco realized that until the employees understood how its finances worked, they would be handicapped in their abilities to help Semco through the financial crisis.

If employees don't understand how money is made or lost, how effectively can they help you make more of it or save it?

In Semco's early years, their financial statements (both at the parent and division levels) were typical for a big company – opaque and confusing, unless you're a professional accountant. There was no way the employees would be able to interpret Semco's finances at a level that would help them act.

In order to address this problem, Semco also simplified profit-and-loss statements to make them more relevant and comprehensible to employees.

It quickly realized that in addition to opening its books to employees, it would also have to teach employees how to understand them, even the simplified versions. The lessons included some fun illustrations and cartoon drawings to make them more interesting and engaging.

Semco's employees were able to see more clearly how their individual and team efforts fit into Semco's operations.

The result? Semco's employees were able to see more clearly how their individual and team efforts fit into Semco's operations and how they could make more money themselves (through profit-sharing), by increasing Semco's profitability.

If your employees don't understand your own finances or finance in general, how effective will be at helping your company make and save more money?

Letting Employees Set Their Own Salaries

Semler believes this is Semco's most controversial practice: letting employees set their own compensation. Naysayers are quick to believe the worst in people, that they will overpay themselves and abuse the system.

That could happen if this isn't done thoughtfully or implemented in a culture that isn't ready for it.

But in the right environment and culture, it works.

Personal salary adjustment isn't for all employees, however, and Semco first developed it in the middle management groups and then began spreading it to other types of employees.

There are five things you need to know in order to set salaries effectively:

1. What other companies are paying for similar roles.

2. What employees with similar jobs and comparable responsibilities inside the company are making.

3. What the division or unit can afford (does it have above- or below-average performance).

4. What the employee would like to be making at this point in his life and career?

5. What the employee's spouse, friends, schoolmates, etc. are making.

Semco actually publishes the information in the first three categories above, which is information that Semco has access to. The employee has access to types 4 and 5. This means the employee has the best perspective to set their compensation at a level they regard as fair.

To safeguard unreasonable salary requests, there are feedback mechanisms, and anyone who requests too large a raise runs the risk of being rejected by their colleagues (compensation is published). Peer pressure is much stronger than any rulebook.

Open compensation policies also reinforce the importance of ensuring that employees understand how the financials and the business work.

With financial literacy, people also get to understand the budget limitations and financial goals of their unit, and can align the incentives with the unit.

Every individual is motivated differently and has different needs.

Every individual is motivated differently and has different needs. That's why Semco has created a bunch of options for how people can choose to take their compensation: fixed salaries, commissions, profit sharing, royalties on profits or revenue, stock or stock options, commissions on gross margin, etc., so that people can truly align what they want with what works for Semco.

Profit Sharing

Semco has a profit sharing plan in which employees can invest part of their compensation. Semco shares on average, 23% of its profit in the plan. 23% is not a magic number, it is a number they came up with after years of trial-and-error experimentation.

Semler shares the story of one of their mechanical assembly technicians named Francisco Alves Pereira. Francisco might invest 2/3 of his raises into the profit sharing plan, and if the goals are met, he'll get back the equivalent of three extra paychecks.

If the unit's goals aren't met, Francisco loses the extra income he would have received from raises (the equivalent of about 10 percent of his income).

You can imagine that Francisco is completely committed to helping the unit make its numbers. He knows the unit's numbers and finances better than most executives and is intimately familiar with production costs. He decides which equipment will be assembled, how and when, to maximize profit.

Francisco wins when the unit wins and is empowered to help it succeed as a mini-CEO.

Job Rotation

Encouraging employees to work in different areas of the business is a phenomenal way to build a company's talent. Here are four valuable reasons to let people, as Semler would say, "ramble" in the company:

- They will have more opportunities to find a place where they are a perfect fit, and can best put their talents to use for the company.

- Your people will understand a bigger picture of the customer lifecycle, rather than a single, narrow job-based view.

- They will enjoy their work more, because they will be learning new things and have new challenges.

- They will help energize the people around them with a new energy, and vitalize thinking and habits that carry deadweight.

The usual reason why <u>managers</u> don't want employees to change jobs: because short-term results might be missed. Yes, sometimes that might happen when an employee moves; but sometimes you might be surprised at the better results or benefits you'll reap by moving people around. Consider it a long-term investment in your company.

Step back and think on if you had encouraged your employees to rotate a year ago, and now, a year later, they know how multiple areas of the company work in attracting and support customers. How much more insightful and productive would they be now at solving problems or generating useful ideas? A lot!

A foundational principle of lean manufacturing and Toyota's success is training employees for different jobs. The employees become better problem-solvers as they gain a broad awareness of how different parts of the business fit together, and they can always be productive at any task no matter what kind of work is needed at that moment.

If you want to turn your employees into mini-CEOs, they have to understand how the business works. There's no better way to achieve that understanding than by working in different parts of the company, whether as a long-term move, a rotation or as a temporary swap with someone.

For example, I guarantee your revenue will go up and arguments will stop if you make your VP Sales and VP Marketing swap roles for a month!

The "Out of Your Mind!" Committee

One of the places employees can bring ideas that aren't a good fit for formal meetings is the "Out of Your Mind!" committee. This is the place to share crazy ideas that might not turn out to be so crazy!

The intention is to create a safe and encouraging place to share ideas based on liberty, respect for others, the power of sharing, and the "sacred right of indolence."

However, the idea should be crazy enough to get the other people on the committee to say, "You're Out of Your Mind!" and to get them to stop, think, and challenge their assumptions.

Even if the idea doesn't turn into a concrete program, it will still spark others' creativity and innovation.

If you don't encourage your employees' ideas, even ones you think are unrealistic or stupid, you'll discourage them from sharing any ideas at all.

At Salesforce.com, I found all my crazier ideas were consistently rejected out-of-hand without much consideration. I quickly learned that it was a waste of time to bring up new ideas and share them unless they were conventional and normal. So I stopped sharing my more interesting ones, the kinds of ideas that might lead to future breakthroughs.

Employees aren't stupid. Why should they share ideas on how to improve the business if others aren't open to those ideas? One person's crazy idea today could be what morphs into a new big idea tomorrow.

"Retire-A-Little"

In your youth and middle-age, you have money and health, but no time. When you're older, you have time and money but no health.

Why can't work be aligned to support this fact of life so that people can have more time when they have their health and so that they can work more in their later years? Semco actually designed a way to support this with the "Retire-A-Little" program. The idea is that you can start enjoying parts of your retirement once a week, from any age.

The program allows the person to do what they plan to do when they retire, once a week, like an art course. They can play sports in the afternoon or spend the day with their kids. In exchange for that time, the company reduces your take-home pay a bit.

This is an experimental program, one that Semler says they don't "know how we'll deal with the offshoot issues that this program may raise…I could think of many reasons to hesitate, as I could have for every one of the thirty of so innovative ideas we have put in place over the last two decades. Nevertheless, 'Retire-A-Little' is chiefly designed to push boundaries and test the future today."

Do you really have to have everything figured out before you try something? Experiment. Perhaps you jumped into starting your company before you knew all the answers.

Find ways to encourage employees to experiment and to develop their entrepreneurial habits into habits of mini-CEO.

"Date Semco"

Semco believes it's important to meet great people who could become valuable employees today or in the future, even if there aren't any current opportunities.

Having great talent is the key to success. But a company doesn't always have an opening for someone it likes, or perhaps that person isn't ready to move yet.

So, Semco created "Date Semco," which allows people to experience what working for Semco is like and allows Semco to get to know prospective hires.

As an example of Semco's innovative hiring ideas, there was a time when Semco needed new blood but couldn't afford to increase the payroll. Semco advertised that while it had no current openings, it would show interested people around the company for a day and accept proposals for a way to work with Semco (for a fee, commission, subcontracting, percentages, by the job, etc.)

Of the hundreds of people visiting their factories, 35 submitted proposals, and two were hired.

One of the proposals was from a man who could help overhaul Semco's machinery to improve efficiencies. He suggested a "success fee," or a percentage of the money saved in operating costs. (This was in the days before outsourcing was popular.)

This job and method was so successful that they applied outsourcing to many other areas of their business.

Before the term "crowd-sourcing" existed, Semco practiced the benefits of being experimental with their recruiting and opening themselves to new ideas, possibilities, and people.

Semco Board Meetings: Are You Serious?

Semco's board has eight seats. Two are reserved for employees who sign up on a first-come, first-serve basis. Yes, those are seats with votes.

This ensures the board doesn't become too isolated from the day-to-day operations of the company. Boards are known in the corporate world for being gatherings of overdressed, overpaid, overly serious white males that don't challenge the CEO enough.

The full breakdown is: Ricardo Semler gets one seat; current executives get three; two spots rotate among senior managers; the last two are the first-come first-served seats, which could be filled by anyone, even a janitor.

Everyone at the meeting has an equal voice. Nothing is confidential.

What better way to give employees a voice and put the board's feet to the fire to ensure the way they make decisions is transparent and logical, so that the company as a whole will understand them and benefit from them?

Obviously if your company is public this isn't going to work exactly like this! But take in the spirit of the practice and find ways to shift your board meetings and culture towards it. How can you bring the voices of your employees and customers into more direct contact with the boardroom?

Most investor-dominated boards will have problems with board openness, because investors tend to be from conventional backgrounds and favor what's worked it the past in business: secrecy and control. The job of a professional investor is (rightly) only about making money, and so unless they see a direct connection with a new business practice and more money, they will resist it.

If you're a CEO who wants to turn your employees into mini-CEOs, be careful about whom you choose as an investor. Find ones who align with your values and culture vision in addition to your market vision.

Keep Opening Up, Patiently & Persistently

As a CEO, try experimenting and testing how much openness your people and board are ready to handle. Test where the right balance lies with your company and culture. Avoid drastic changes that will cause more disturbance than benefit. Push and stretch for a little more openness than what is currently comfortable, but not too much.

As people adapt, keep pushing for more openness – patiently and persistently. It takes time for people – whether board members or employees – to adapt to anything new.

(Want to see more examples of Semco's policies? See Appendix B: *Semco Employee Survival Guide*)

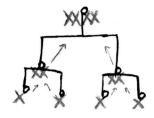

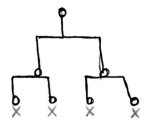

COMMAND + CONTROL

- Every problem escalated
- Decisions pushed up

CEOFLOW

- Problems solved at source
- Decisions pushed down

Decision-making is one of the most important skills a CEO, or mini-CEO, needs. It is like a muscle – it requires regular exercise to stay in shape.

Do your people have to get approval for everything from managers? Does your company thus discourage its people from making their own decisions and taking responsibility?

The more your company culture requires employees to get managers to approve decisions (through explicit or implicit rules), the more you are training employees to not make decisions for themselves, and you are clogging managers' time.

Here is how problems can multiply: let's say a customer support person has a problem with a customer, and that they aren't trained or empowered to resolve this kind of problem on their own.

The customer support person must ask their manager for help or approval in resolving the problem. Now you have twice as many people who have problems to deal with – the customer support person and the manager.

Push down decisions as low as you can, even if you have to change your processes and increase your training.

Rather than getting *approval* for a decision from a manager or executive, set a rule that people must only ask for *advice* from a manager or executive (or peers) before making their own decisions. Have them practice their decision-making habits, even if they make some wrong ones at first.

The more your people own their own decisions, and practice making their own decisions, the more easily they will develop into mini-CEOs.

(For the full-color version of this and more sketches, go to www.CEOFlow.com/sketches)

7

Case Study: AES

The primary factor in determining whether people experience joy or drudgery in the workplace is the degree to which they control their work, which primarily means making decisions and taking responsibility for them.
~ *Dennis Bakke*

In addition to Semler's *The Seven Day Weekend,* the second book I've found with the best specific examples of how to turn your employees into mini-CEOs is Dennis Bakke's *Joy At Work.*

Bakke founded AES with a partner in 1982. By 2002, only 20 years later, AES was an $8.6 billion dollar energy company with 40,000 worldwide employees. Unfortunately AES was caught in the energy market cataclysms of 2002 and went under, along with many other energy companies at that time.

However, that doesn't diminish his story of how he turned his employees into mini-CEOs in order to create a multi-billion company.

Joy At Work is packed with stories, principles, and ideas. Two practices in the book are the most relevant to developing mini-CEOs: 1) AES' decision-making process and 2) their "Honeycomb" organizational structure.

I Love AES' Elegant Decision-Making System

"Before any decision can be made on any company matter,
the decision maker must seek advice."

~ *Dennis Bakke*

One of AES' simplest and most effective practices was their decision-making system. It might sound simple at first, but it has some elegant twists.

First, every decision had a single, designated decision maker. There might have been committees to assist in the process, but ultimately a single person made each decision.

Second, that person was whoever was best positioned to make the decision, regardless of how high or low they were in the company. In fact, AES pushed important decisions down as low as possible.

Leaders had to let go of most of their traditional responsibility and power of making most of the decisions. One of their reactions at first was, "Isn't that what we're paid for?" Actually, an even more valuable use of their experience was to coach employees on making their own decisions.

Third, the decision-maker made the decision for the whole company. Once the decision was made, the company had to support it without second-guessing.

That means a person on a team in a plant could make a decision that could materially affect the whole company, such as with an environmental or regulatory situation. Talk about training people how to make decisions and take responsibility!

To be able to empower individuals on the line at that level but without endangering the company, AES created their "advice process," a simple yet controversial process.

Instead of a boss asking advice from subordinates and peers before making a decision, the decision maker – who was almost never one of the executives or officials – seeks advice from leaders and peers and anyone who might be affected by the decision.

Usually the decision maker is the person most affected by the decision, or who initiates the idea, discovers a problem, or otherwise has the most engagement with the situation.

Before the decision can be made the decision-maker must seek advice, and the larger the issue, the wider the net they must cast.

Five important things happen when this advice-gathering process is followed:

- **First**, it engages the people most likely to be affected by the decision. They have an awareness of the issue and feel their voice is heard.

- **Second**, asking for advice is a process of humility and forges stronger relationships across the team and company. Instead of an "I don't need you" attitude of isolationism, common in western corporate cultures, it fosters one of communication and teamwork.

- **Third**, one of THE most important skills of a mini-CEO is decision- making. It is like a sport, in that a person gets better with practice. If you don't give your people a chance to practice making decisions, they won't be as effective at them.

- **Fourth**, better decisions are made because they are being made by the person closest to the issue. Decision-by-committee is avoided. Have you heard the phrase, "A camel is a horse designed by committee"?

- **Fifth**, the decision maker has more fun with work because they're controlling their own destiny. Bakke believes the amount of fun in an organization is largely a function of how many decisions the people get to make. Making decisions also stimulates creativity and talent.

"More often than not, lower-ranking people are closer to the problem and better positioned to come up with a solution." ~ Dennis Bakke

AES' "Honeycomb" Organizational Structure

AES' structure, while not as radical as Semco's, was unconventional and put many people who saw it as radically different, "out of control," undisciplined, and uncoordinated. That is, it wasn't "under control" (aka "Push Management").

AES' Honeycomb structure began after Bakke's intense frustration he experienced while helping managers of their Houston plant draft a new employee handbook. As people kept discussing all the possible situations employees can get into, especially around "leave policy" and sick days, the handbook quickly became longer and longer.

Bakke wondered why they needed a handbook at all – couldn't AES trust people to use their best judgment? (This was before Nordstrom became famous for their single customer service rule: "Use good judgment in all situations.")

Bakke's partner, Roger Sant, expressed it this way: "When you are sick, stay at home. You don't need a handbook to tell you when or how long you can be sick or what you should do about it."

This led Bakke to begin questioning other aspects of their management systems.

- What if they eliminated the handbook? (No one looks at them anyway.)
- What if they ditched the detailed job descriptions?
- What if they eliminated shift supervisors, and let go of having to have detailed org chart boxes to stick people into?
- What if people had no written spending limits?
- What if they created teams of people around areas of the plant to operate and maintain the facility, instead of letting bosses assign tasks and run the plant?
- What if each team set its own hours and schedule?

Reminds you of Ricardo Semler's "always ask why?" philosophy, right?

This line of thinking led to what Bakke described as a Honeycomb system. The "Honeycomb" name was inspired by a story his uncle told him about bees. The bees in a beehive operate independently, but in a coordinated fashion, to go out and find food to bring back to the hive.

Similar to an ant colony, each individual bee is empowered to act on their own to contribute as mini-CEO bees.

The Houston plant ended up reorganizing themselves into the Honeycomb theme by blowing up the hierarchical model (getting rid of two supervisory layers) and creating seven new teams (called "families"), around major business functions, not tasks.

For example, there was a Boiler family, and Environmental Cleanup family, a Turbine Facility family, and others. Each was designed to be as self-managing as possible. They had a team leader who reported to the plant manager and who would be responsible for their own budgets, schedules, compensation, expenditures, purchasing, quality control, and other functions.

Each 'family' was run like a mini-business, which of course required the people and team leaders to develop themselves as mini-CEOs.

AES employees now could learn how to make better overall business decisions because they were working more closely in alignment with the actual business. Now, each employee could see directly how their scheduling, purchasing, and quality control financially impacted their mini-business, and thus AES.

After it succeeded in Houston, AES spread this style of management throughout the company.

After it succeeded in Houston, AES spread this style of management throughout the company. They created collections of small, interacting groups of multi-skilled employees. Individuals in a team might have to juggle varied responsibilities such as investments, day-to-day operations, hiring and firing, scheduling, safety, risk management, education or environmental management, charitable giving or community relations.

Bakke continued to work to empower these kinds of mini-businesses and to reduce corporate staff of budgeting analysts, long-term planners, safety experts, HR, and IT. He felt these corporate staffers don't fully appreciate or understand the operating groups and their problems. The specialists are too disconnected from the field.

While forming these multi-tasking self-managing teams does involve the loss of specialization, individuals in the teams gain the benefits of broader understanding of how the business works, how to solve problems, closer teamwork, and more ownership over the business results.

Blowing Up Spending Rules

A casualty of the Honeycomb system was preset spending limits for employees. Previously, spending limits were set at tiered levels such as $100,000 for a plant manager, $10,000 for unit leaders, $1,000 for others, and so on.

AES eliminated ALL of those predefined spending limits! The only rule was that employees making decisions on expenditures had to ask advice of more senior people before acting.

Dennis Bakke's Comparison Of "Conventional" And "Joy At Work" Approaches

One of my favorite sections of his book is an appendix in which he compares side-by-side the conventional approach and the *Joy At Work* approach. It's worth buying the book just to get that section. Here are some highlights:

A Conventional Approach	The Joy At Work Approach
95%+ of the important decisions are made by the official leaders (executives, board members).	99% of all important decisions are made by non-leaders.
Decisions are forced as high as practical for approval.	Decisions are pushed down to be made at the lowest practical levels.
Employees have fixed expenditure limits, beyond which they need higher-level approval.	Employees have no cap or required approval process on spending money – only getting advice prior towards spending is mandatory.
Leaders see their role as managing people and resources.	Leaders see their role as serving other employees.
A structure of job positions, roles, and titles that don't change much over time.	No company-wide job descriptions. Every person is considered unique and builds a description around their passions and talents.
Management and line workers are treated and paid differently, creating rifts.	There is only one category of employee; there are no managers.

Bakkes "Top 10" For Joy At Work At AES

1. When given the opportunity to use our ability to reason, make decisions and take responsibility for our actions, we experience joy at work.

2. The purpose of business is not to maximize profit to shareholders but to steward our resources to serve the world in an economically sustainable way.

3. Attempt to create the most fun workplace in the history of the world.

4. Eliminate management, organization charts, job descriptions, and hourly wages.

5. Fairness means treating everyone differently.

6. Principles and values must guide all decisions.

7. Put other stakeholders (shareholders, customers, suppliers, etc.) equal to or above yourself.

8. Everyone must get advice before making a decision. If you don't seek advice, you're fired.

9. A "good" decision should make all the stakeholders unhappy because no individual or group got all they wanted.

10. Lead with passion, humility, and love.

A Vision For Honeycomb in Technology and Business Services Companies

Can Honeycomb work in the technology and business services industries? I haven't seen it anywhere yet, but I don't see why it can't. It was way too radical for Salesforce.com to even consider. I wish Salesforce.com had a "You Gotta Be Crazy!" committee like Semco!

I'm a big fan of lean manufacturing and the Toyota Way – it has revolutionized manufacturing in this century (I list two books about it in the Resources Chapter).

Toyota has "flow" down to an art form in their systems, which has enabled them to become the most successful car company in the world.

I have a vision for technology companies, one that is already working in some other kinds of services and manufacturing companies.

The management practices of most business-to-business technology and business services industries are in many ways like the manufacturing practices of the giants-of-old (General Motors) who were surpassed by the lean giants-of-new (Toyota).

I want to see the management models of companies evolve towards AES' Honeycomb model, like a collection of "businesses inside a bigger business". Rather than being divided into teams based purely on function (Sales, Marketing Services), employees are grouped into mini-business units that include a variety of functional roles in each team.

For example, what if, instead of having massive and distinct teams of people just doing sales, or only doing support, or only marketing... you remixed those employees into mini-business units similar to a retail chain that composed of lots of mini-businesses (retail stores)?

Say you're a software company. What if you created a "pod-team" mini-business structure with its own territory that included, just as an example, one marketing person, two inside salespeople, two outside salespeople, an account manager, two support people, and a technical expert/sales engineer?

What if each person in that mini-business could learn about customer needs and experiences from each other? Imagine your sales guy, after he's been through basic sales training with other salespeople, is sitting next to a marketing person and a support person...

Wouldn't the salesperson how to sell more effectively by learning from the marketing and support persons how to speak in the customers' language, avoid problem customers, set expectations, get more referrals and win more deals?

Wouldn't the marketing person learn how to market more effectively by hearing the salesperson sell and by learning from the support person how customers actually use the product?

Wouldn't the support person head off more issues early before they fester, because they've been able to observe the lifecycle of the customer from when they entered the sales cycle?

What if you measured and compensated the mini-businesses on metrics that completely align with your company's key metrics, such as Revenue, Profitability, and ROI of their mini-business?

What if one of the team was a mini-CEO, who ran the team like a general manager of a retail store or division and managed the financial profit and loss statement of his mini-business, hiring, firing, coaching, customer satisfaction and sales?

Can you imagine the kind of talented people you could develop this way, people who could truly be mini-CEOs in your business and help take it to the next level without needing you to hold their hands?

I know someone out there is doing something like this in technology or other high-value services businesses. I would love to hear from you - reach out and share your system and story and what is working or not working with it!

Contact me through www.CEOFlow.com or email: info@pebblestorm. com

Sketch: "Cake Sketch" (The CEO Is The Pebble In The Pond)

The CEO sets the tone of the company. Are you creating a culture of fear and stress, or of trust and inspiration? What is trickling down to your customers?

For example, a CEO hammers on the VP Sales for results...

Who hammers on a sales person for results...

Who annoys prospects and clients for deals...

The deals might come in this month, but what is the long-term damage to the relationship from pressuring, cajoling, or just irritating customers?

(For the full-color version of this and more sketches, go to www.CEOFlow.com/sketches)

8

The Three Core CEOFlow Values of Trust, Transparency And Alignment

"Employees will not trust a company more than the company trusts them."
~ Aaron Ross

There are three fundamental management values or operating principles that a CEO and managers can take to heart to help shift their culture away from push and closer to pull: **Trust, Transparency and Alignment.** The CEO must be the one to lead by example in creating this kind of environment.

You know your company is getting closer to "Pull" when when the drama, confusion, and wasted energy go down, and the synergy, "we're getting things done" feeling, and seemingly effortless growth go up.

Management Values Leading To CEOFlow

1. TRUST

If there is one thing that would get rid of the internal cultural blocks on your growth, it's more trust.

Consider all the time we spend on issues related to lack of trust: controlling policies, tracking systems, "what are you doing?" meetings, contracts that are far too long and complex, constant second-guessing, internal gossip and

101

drama…what a damn WASTE! None of this leads to growth, and it's a pain in everyone's ass. Some needs to stay but how much of it can you let go of?

Keep in mind: *employees will not trust a company more than the company trusts them.* If you want your people to trust you and the company, the CEO and management team have to lead by example, even in little ways.

For example, next time someone comes to you with an idea that you disagree with or want done differently, don't automatically say "no" or tell them what to do. Try letting them explore it and see what happens. Even if it doesn't go anywhere, they'll be a little more motivated and appreciative of you.

Start with little steps and keep at it. Trust takes time to build, and is easily lost.

2. TRANSPARENCY

Transparency is a modern form of truth. "Truth" is relative to everyone, but transparency is absolute.

Transparency prevents miscommunication and confusion, improves decisions across the company, and increases trust.

How much of what you feel should be secret really has to be? What is the cost of hiding information from your employees?

What would be the benefit of having them know more about what's going on and trusting the company more?

Let the paranoia go.

The next chapter digs further into transparency, with examples on how to begin increasing it without upsetting the boat too much.

3. ALIGNMENT

Having all these motivated people doesn't help much if they're all working at cross-purposes.

Alignment means more than having common goals; it means asking whether there is a common vision and if *everyone understand it.* As a CEO, founder, or executive, it's very common to assume that everyone gets it because you do. The most common problem with communication is *assuming it happened.*

- Do people work under a common set of values?
- Is there a common (aligned) culture?
- Does the team feel like it's in the same boat with the executives, or do the executives set themselves apart with a variety of perks and special treatments?

(FYI – I'm a believer in blowing up executive offices, because they hurt transparency, communication, and alignment. As an investor in companies, I want the CEO to get the hell out of his office and work among his people, so that he's in constant sync with them. It's the right *business decision.*)

As the goals change, sometimes by the week or month, is that information transparently propagated through the company so that everyone can update their own and stay aligned? Wikis, company dashboards and regular company updates or offsites are all useful methods to widely share information.

Positive Feedback Loops & Baby Steps

These three fundamental values of trust, transparency and alignment are synergistic. Increasing one increases the others. Increasing transparency = increased trust and alignment. Increased alignment = more trust.

You can't create an environment of trust and total transparency overnight. It takes time. Start with small steps. My advice: share more about yourself and what is going on in the business. Share more than what is comfortable, but not so much that it is very uncomfortable.

9

The Power of Transparency

"Those who hoard information are attempting to accumulate power."

~ Ricardo Semler

You can only turn your employees into mini-CEOs if you distribute & delegate power. Transparency, even more than what you are comfortable with today, is vital to this. Except for a few truly sensitive topics such as margin data, unique materials or technology sources, or future product plans, most of what you keep confidential from employees doesn't have to be.

For example, why do you keep your financial information secret? Have you ever really thought about it?

If you're worried that sharing your financials with employees will make it easy for competitors to get a hold of them, so what? What is the worst that can happen if competitors did get hold of your financials? By the way, if you ask employees not to share information with other people and you tell them WHY they shouldn't, they will be much more careful than if you just tell them to keep it confidential without explaining why.

Consider the benefit of employees who know how your finances work and can be more engaged and knowledgeable about how to help improve them!

What Would It Take To Get "Naked"?

Usually transparency is a problem when there is something to hide – a lack of fairness or things (goals, comp, plans, directives) that are arbitrary. So before you increase transparency, you might have to fix some things behind the scenes.

Share board updates with the whole company after every meeting. Publish financials internally. Do CEO updates every week. Put webcams up in executive meetings. Just try it and see the effect it has on your people and their motivation!

Okay, wait – remember that big changes (in transparency or other areas) often aren't sustainable for you or employees. Changes stick when done in baby steps, over time and with commitment. So if getting naked is too big a leap right now, just start with a first step, and build from there. Keep it simple and keep at it.

A Simple Example Of How I Used Transparency With My Sales Team's Compensation

As I described in my chapter about Salesforce.com, I published the compensation of everyone on my sales team (this wasn't a practice across the company), so that:

- They could verify the comp calculations were correct (reducing payroll errors and frustrations).
- They could see where they stood and whom they should be emulating.
- It increased transparency and trust in the team.
- They could help me revise the compensation system to improve it.

Now, this kind of comp transparency won't work well if your comp plans vary per person or aren't fair - usually because of special deals or arbitrary plans.

People talk about comp anyway, so it's always best if you can avoid doing things in the first place that you don't want to be discovered.

This kind of transparent comp practice forces you to make your comp planning sustainable, fair, and without arbitrariness. Avoid special tricks or custom compensation deals for people, ESPECIALLY in sales. Arbitrary compensation plans are corrosive to companies because it reduces trust and increases jealousness.

Different comp plans and amounts are fine if there are rational reasons for them that you can explain to people so they understand "the why" behind them.

Examples Of Using Transparency To Improve Trust And Productivity

Here are some examples and results of conversations I've had with different CEOs on how the implement transparency and some of the issues they consider or worry about.

1) More transparency is better with investors and the board. Transparency is essential to building trust, and if your board doesn't trust you or your executives, you have a serious problem.

Transparency, including getting real about problems and never sugarcoating the truth, is vital to building the trust necessary to both raise money from investors and to maintain their support after they've invested.

There should be direct board-to-executive team interaction to increase trust and communication with the team beyond the CEO. Individual executives should regularly prepare and present to the board, rather than have all information flow through the CEO.

2) More transparency (perhaps than you're comfortable with) is better with employees. For example, sharing your board presentations to the company is a great way to regularly update the company on what's going on.

Frank Addante, CEO of Rubicon Project and a leading serial entrepreneur in LA, writes about why he does this:

> *"I like to hold monthly board meetings. They serve two purposes. First, regular communication with the board. Second, regular communication with the entire team because we share the same board of directors meeting presentation with the entire team (yes, really — exactly the same.)*

> *This is much easier said than done. It forces a certain discipline. For example, I cannot tell the board something that the team is not already aware of (e.g. problem areas in the company or concerns) because I know we'll be sharing those same exact slides with the entire team.*

Vice-versa, I can't tell the board something that the entire team wouldn't agree with because they are living this business everyday. If the team saw something in the board slides that they didn't agree with, I wouldn't be able to stand up and present it to them with a straight face.

It forces complete alignment with everyone in the company all the way through to the board."

3) Have a goal of "No Surprises" – I personally love this as a fundamental operating and management principle. No one, including the CEO, employees, customers, or investors like surprises.

- What would it take to have a company in which no one is surprised? Neither the CEO, employees, clients nor partners.
- What kinds of systems would you have to create for customers and internal operations?

4) Transparency with employees builds trust, increases retention and improves decision-making. Employees also feel more connected to the business (I would suggest this is true of being transparent with clients as well).

I know that one of my biggest frustrations at companies was the lack of transparency. If a company isn't going to share or invest with me, why should I share or invest in them beyond the bare minimum?

As described in the chapter on Semco, Semco's decision to open it books and become financially transparent helped its employees understand its business better and the employees felt more engaged with the business.

The employees were then in a much better and more motivated position to go above and beyond their normal duties in order to contribute to the company's results.

5) Comp idea: standardize the executive team. One idea that generated "that's cool" comments from a group of CEOs was the practice of having the whole executive team on the same comp plan structure (decided and designed by the executive team as a group).

This means everyone is in the same boat, and transparency and alignment become easier.

Whether or not this works past the startup stage will depend on the CEO and the culture. If a company pursues a classical function-based hierarchy

(VP of Sales, VP Marketing, etc), then market demands will probably twist your arm to customize compensation per role.

If you go a route in which leaders don't have those kinds of fixed narrow responsibilities, such as with the Honeycomb structure of AES, you have a higher probability of being able have one comp structure that most people share.

6) Publishing compensation: this is tricky if it's not done from the beginning and if the comp system itself isn't fair.

Don't feel obligated to publish compensation information. However, if you decide to do it, start a conversation with your employees (not just executives) about it and how to do it in a way that minimizes disruption. Don't just drop it on the company out of the blue. Remember, people don't like surprises!

If sharing more information about compensation is intimidating, consider sharing more information about the different ways your employees are rewarded. Start educating employees on how compensation works.

What are the structures, criteria, processes? How were the compensation systems designed? If it was arbitrary, then get a group of employees together as a team to create systems around compensation so that people understand how the systems work before you start to share compensation data itself.

People focus on inequalities when those inequalities are arbitrary or they don't understand why they exist.

People focus on inequalities when those inequalities are arbitrary or they don't understand why they exist.

If you have a rationale for difference in compensation that make sense to people, they'll be ok AND they'll have a clearer path to understanding what it will take for them to increase their value to the company and be able to earn more.

To publish comp information, it must be done in the right environment, carefully, and the comp system must already be fair *before* publishing. Here is the test: if the comp were made public: could the CEO stand up and justify the system and each person's comp?

Publishing an "unfair" system that can't be reasonably justified will cause pure chaos.

It could be published piecemeal, just within certain functions or teams. For example, I openly published comp results across my sales team at Salesforce.com every month.

According to an article titled "Why Do You Keep Your Salary Secret?"

> *It's really a fairly narrow band of Americans who have secrecy with respect to their pay. Obviously, at the very top of organizations, pay is public. If you look at public-sector organizations—it's public. If you look at unionized situations—it's public. If you look at most people who are nonexempt employees—it's public. It's really that middle ground in private-sector organizations where secrecy is seen as the right way to manage.*

(Blog post by Alexander Kjerulf: "Why Secret Salaries Are A Baaaaad Idea": http://positivesharing.com/2006/08/why-secret-salaries-are-a-baaaaaad-idea

Rebuttals and comments to Alex's post: "The Case Against Open Salaries": http://positivesharing.com/2006/08/the-case-against-open-salaries)

7) Financial transparency / open books: Regularly publishing financial information, down to the lowest employees, can be hugely beneficial to a business.

Mike Rosenthal has a helpful personal example from his days as CEO at Siteler Wash (www.sitelerwash.com) an onsite car washing business. Siteler published the P&L every week to the people washing the cars, even though the car washers often needed Spanish translators and as well as help understanding the financials. Siteler saw a productivity increase within *two weeks*, because car washers began to see more clearly how they fit in financially and how they could contribute. They also felt more connected to the business. Productivity ultimately grew by 30-40%!

Ian Shea (founder, MaestroMarket, an online platform and marketplace connecting professionals who have specialized talent with customers in need of that talent) shares a daily "flash" of business metrics with his people to inform them of a daily progress drumbeat.

Semco, as I wrote about in an earlier chapter, has totally open books to its employees, and has regular training classes for anyone (including janitors) who wants to learn how to understand the finances. The company also takes pains to present the financials in simplified ways that are meaningful to employees.

8) Transparency with cashflow problems: It's scary to run low on cash, making it hard to feel comfortable letting the whole company know about it. However, I believe that you should be transparent with your people even when you're struggling.

If you've been keeping the situation close to the vest, don't just dump scary news on people with no warning. You have to warm them up first.

One example argument for keeping cashflow problems secret goes like this: if a team feels confident about raising the money and the cashflow problem will disappear, why unnecessarily spook your people?

Rather, I would tell you to share openly: if you were an employee at a company running low on cash, wouldn't you want to know? And people will probably know about it anyway – word gets around.

Follow the Golden Rule: if you were working for your company, what would you want to know, and when?

Also, if you let the whole company know about issues as serious even as a cash crisis, you then have an opportunity to rally the entire company to help navigate the crisis. You might lose some people, but the people left behind will be the strong core.

At LeaseExchange, as cash ran low, we were very open about our cash issues and plans. Some people did leave, but the people who stayed formed a strong, tight core. Work was much more fun and productive when we slimmed down to the group of people that were most committed to the cause.

As with all of the guidance I'm sharing here, you always must use your best judgment in what to try yourself, and how. For example, too much transparency too fast could be a business-threatening move if it could threaten existing bank loans or lines of credit in some way.

Transparent Selling & Account Management

Transparent selling. Are sales organizations and people ready for a "transparent sales process"? (I have one, contact me through www.CEOFlow.com or info@pebblestorm.com for the template.)

Example: Leads360, a software-as-a-service company in Los Angeles, put up a version of it on their website at: www.leads360.com/process.

More transparency with customers. Sharing more information with customers, whether openly on your website or in more targeted ways, will increase their trust and appreciation of your company. You can share anything from event schedules to product roadmaps, customer lists, uptime information, current business priorities and goals, etc.

Example: www.trust.salesforce.com, which was a BIG deal for Salesforce.com to publish this In the first place. Because of competitive/sales reasons, for years Salesforce.com was extremely secretive about its uptime performance. Salesforce.com only decided to publish them transparently when repeated downtime problems and opacity increased customer distrust.)

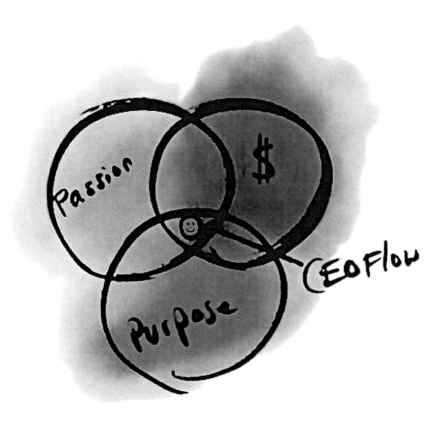

Sketch: CEO Sweet Spot

The CEO is the person who sends the ripples out through the company that will inspire or de-motivate people. To maintain a productive and energizing environment, we need you (the CEO) to stay in a sweet spot as much as possible, so that you can inspire employees and customers just by being who you are.

(For the full-color version of this and more sketches, go to www.CEOFlow.com/sketches)

10

The CEOFlow System

"A leader is best when people barely know that he exists."

~ Witter Bynner

CEOFlow is the systematization of what I and the other founders of freedom companies like Semco, AES, and others have created intuitively. It includes:

- A step-by-step CEOFlow System
- Individual and group coaching programs
- A community of like-minded peers
    - ° Enhanced with fun, creativity- and community-inducing adventures for CEOs and teams!

This section includes some examples of the foundational principles underlying CEOFlow. For the expanded content on these principles and the CEOFlow System, go to www.CEOFlow.com to read or download extra free chapters.

Five Myths About Getting The Most Out Of Your Employees

1. You must always seem strong, in control, and have all the answers
2. Employees don't need to (and shouldn't) know everything that's going on in the business

115

3. You have to sacrifice a lot of your own enjoyment and fun for your business to succeed

4. Mistakes and failures are bad

5. The more you work, the more successful the business will be

Your Role As CEO

- Transparency
- Openness
- Supportive
- Forgiving/Accepting
- Direct & Clear
- Committed, But Not Attached ("Have a plan and hold it lightly")

Seven Golden Rules In Creating An Employee-Led Workplace

1. You work for your employees – they do not work for you
2. Create a culture of no surprises and no blame
3. Let go of those who don't belong
4. Allow your employees to stumble
5. Take baby steps
6. Get a coach or mentor
7. Find a community of like-minded CEOs

The Step-By-Step CEOFlow System

1. CEO Clarity
2. Choose Your Next Adventure
3. Create A Shared Vision
4. Set Up Your Drumbeat
5. Share The Journey
6. Share The Results

Visit *www.CEOFlow.com* to get free expanded content on these aspects of the CEOFlow System.

Sketch: The CEO's Life Matters

The CEO influences and affects everything around them – both consciously and unconsciously.

If disorder increases in the CEO's life, then at some level – whether minor or painfully obvious – disorder will increase in the company.

If the CEO is centered and focused – the people and company will be more centered and focused.

In that sense, the CEOs need to include their own lives as part of business planning

(For the full-color version of this and more sketches, go to www.CEOFlow.com/sketches)

11

Next Steps You Can Take

"Patience and perseverance have a magical effect before which difficulties disappear and obstacles vanish."

~ John Quincy Adams

"One moment of patience may ward off great disaster. One moment of impatience may ruin a whole life."

~ Chinese Proverb

Where's a good place to begin to take all of these ideas and examples and do something with them?

It begins with you and what your vision is for yourself as a person who is more than just "the CEO." You're not your job. Once you clarify what you want in both life and work, it becomes easier to move forward with the others on your team or to realize that your team needs to change.

Here are some specific suggestions for actions you can take:

1. Reflect on your Ideal Work vision and what your personal, Unique Genius is. Your business is supposed to help you get what you want from life, so get clear on that first.

119

Spend some time writing about and reflecting on your "ideal work", your dream business. If you could create any business, or reshape your current one, how would it feel, what would it look like and do? Consider the purpose of your business and your own personal life purpose.

Start creating a new vision that your business and employees can evolve into over time by answering these questions:

1. Do you want to be a CEO, or do you want a different role at some point?

2. What parts of your work drain you, and what energizes you? What parts of your work do you want to get rid of first?

3. What would be your ideal "day in a life?"

4. Who are your ideal clients? What kinds of clients are toxic?

5. What kinds of people are your ideal employees? Who is toxic?

7. How many hours a week do you want to work?

8. How long do you want to own or be in the business?

9. How many employees do you want to have? Do you want a larger company or a smaller, leaner team? Why? (Bigger and more employees is not necessarily better.)

10. If you could be assured of success at doing ANYTHING (besides being a parent or success in your current business), what would it be? Are you not living up to your potential because you buried some talents, passions, or dreams as your career or business grew?

11. Do you have other passions that you can bring into work? For example, if you love movies, you could help employees produce a short and fun movie about your company to share with potential hires and media outlets.

(I have a "Unique Genius Worksheet" available for downloading for free at www.Pebblestorm.com/updates)

2. Walk around and start talking to employees. If you're the type of leader that ends up getting busy in your office or on the road, just start talking to people again.

The CEOFlow practices and ideas will succeed much more easily when you start with a culture of trust and communication, which can be as simple as talking to more of your people more regularly.

3) Start a regularly scheduled "Meeting Of The Minds" event, in which ANY and all employees are encouraged to come and share ideas that will help improve the business or make the culture more fun and magnetic to both current and prospective employees.

This won't work if you gather ideas and then do nothing with them. After each meeting, pick just one idea for someone to implement before the next meeting or at least a milestone of the idea if it's a longer term project.

The ideas can be as simple as having a car washer come to your parking lot once a week to make it easy for employees to pay to get their cars washed (as Leads360 did).

Or it could be more complex ideas about new products, better customer service, or how to make more money for the company.

Don't just assign people these ideas as extra work projects. Let people volunteer for what inspires them, and allow them to create it in ways that inspire them and are fun.

4) Try letting some employees stumble, even in client meetings. Sasha Strauss, CEO of Innovation Protocol, a world-class brand strategy consulting firm for the Fortune 500, has shared some great stories with me about how he lets employees stumble safely, even in live sales situations:

- *Sasha will take some junior account people to a meeting with a large client, and tell them ahead of time that it's their meeting to run.*

- *Sasha lets his junior people drive the meeting.*

- *Sasha knows that there is no mistake they can make that he can't fix with a client based on his 14 years of experience in similar meetings.*

- *If the client doesn't react positively to the junior team member, it's just an opportunity for that individual to learn about how to improve for the next time. If it isn't real, people won't really learn.*

If you don't give employees some space to stumble and make mistakes, they aren't going to learn how to be entrepreneurial enough to help run parts of the company for you.

5) Hold transparent monthly company updates where you share your board meeting slides like Frank Addante does, who is CEO of The Rubicon Project (whose work I described in the Power Of Transparency chapter):

- Have a once-a-month company conversation in which you share a full financial and operations update with the company.

- If you don't have regular board meetings or executive meetings in which you regularly step back to reflect on the business, start now!

What if you feel that openly sharing the contents of board meetings is too big a step?

If you aren't holding monthly company updates now, commit to holding one this month even if you're not prepared to share as transparently as Frank.

If you are holding them every few months, do it every month.

Each time you hold a meeting, share a little more. Take baby steps if you need to. Each time, share more than you are comfortable with but not so much that it paralyzes you or causes stress to you or to the company.

For example, if you are in a cash crunch right now, but no one knows except your executive team, don't just dump it on the company. Prepare people for it ahead of time. Remember, people, including yourself, hate surprises. Surprise kills trust, and trust is the bedrock of turning your employees into Mini-CEOs.

6) Survey Employees – how is morale? If your employees are happier, they'll be more motivated, make better mini-CEOs as a whole, and will attract better talent.

This is different and simpler than a 360 performance review process, which gets into the heart of how to help individuals improve. The goal of a morale survey is this simple: to determine whether people are happy or unhappy at work.

Surveying your people doesn't have to be a big project. Here are three ways you can go, from simple to more complex:

a) Walk around the office and ask people how they are – and MEAN IT. Ask one or two people at a time to go out for a walk to get coffee, or call a remote employee. You should do this regularly in any case and with people you don't see every day.

b) Run a simple online survey through a service like SurveyMonkey. com. You can literally begin with something as simple as these three questions in order to get a pulse on your company's morale:

1. "Are you satisfied with working at _____? (Yes/ No/Neutral)"

2. "On a scale of 1-10, how much do you enjoy working at _____?"

3. "Would you recommend to friends that they work at _____?"

c) Run a CEOFlow Survey that is a little more in-depth, with about 20 questions. It's a quick gauge - like using a thermometer to take your body temperature. If the temperature isn't around 98.6 degrees, you may not know what the problem is yet, but at least you know there is a problem.

If you at least know employee morale is lower than you hoped, you can determine what to do about it. See CEOFlow.com for more information.

7) Charge up your culture with an office makeover. Do new recruits get turned off by the lack of personality in your office? Just by adding some color, shifting people around, moving people from offices into common areas and encouraging people to decorate themselves, you can bring up your energy level!

At CEOFlow, when we do a consulting project to help a company make its physical environment more interesting and attractive, we call it giving you a "Culture Charge".

Zappos is famous for this and other ways to make work fun. Search online for "Zappos Inside Blog" to find their blog about their internal culture.

8) Hold offsites that, in interesting and fun ways, align your teams' goals, build teamwork and spark creativity:

- The key here is not to follow the typical offsite route: an executive-only retreat at which people share standard updates on their part of the business and bore everyone else to tears.

- Invite as many people as is practical to attend, or at least more people than you normally would, and go down at least one level in responsibility.

- Have some icebreaker events and games planned into the schedule to loosen up people and to build trust through the teams.

- Have each group share their business goals for the next 6-12 months, and use the "group mind" to refine them and align them with the other teams.

  - This is not a time to try to look good and show off – get real. The CEO and executives must reward transparency and authenticity as much or more than successes.

  - If you only reward successes and not authenticity, people will hide things that aren't working and will burnish things that are just barely working.

- Have each unit share its main challenges.

- Work as a group to create, shape and prioritize solutions.

- Assign each solution a single owner, with milestones.

- Publish this plan openly to the entire company.

- Make it fun!

  - Have some fun events like Damir Davidovic, CEO of NEOGOV, created. He had teams of people do an IronChef-like cooking class and cookoff that his people enjoyed.

  - Damir even took some of the video taken during the offsite and turned it into fun clips he could share with the employees around the world to help inspire people who weren't there in person.

Your Perfect Chance To Practice Co-Creation And No Surprises

Don't get so excited that you hit the accelerator and crash the car.

For example, suddenly publishing all your compensation information in a monthly update without discussing it with the whole company would be a recipe for disaster.

People own what they help create, and no one likes surprises. A perfect way to move forward is to share a list of these kinds of ideas with your employees, and have them help you implement them.

This doesn't mean you have to do what employees say or that you shouldn't push them. Yes, challenge them to step up and get creative together with you!

If you are honest about wanting their help in co-creating something, they will help out wholeheartedly and be inspired by it. If they feel you're just trying to dump more work on them and that you don't, at an emotional level, buy in, they won't give you their best either.

Baby Steps & Patience

No matter what, just take a first step. That is where it begins, and you can't take a first step that is too small.

If you keep on taking those baby steps, while it might feel sometimes that things are moving too slowly, remember that it takes time to change habits and develop people – to create mini-CEOs.

Keep at it and you will look back and be amazed at what you and your mini-CEOs have accomplished!

Sketch: Shift Your Perspective On Work

The way you look at work has a drastic impact on your approach to it, and to your employees' approach to it.

Do you see work in burdensome terms of "I have to do this," or do you see work as a choice? Do you see that you have choices in your work such as whom you work with, how you work, and even how much you work?

Do you see work in terms of "I need to work" or "I want to work"? If you don't want to work, start re-imagining your work to find ways in which you would want to work, in which you'd enjoy it.

Work can be enjoyable and energizing if you consciously design it to be!

(For the full-color version of this and more sketches, go to www.CEOFlow.com/sketches)

Final Word: Stay Committed To Your Vision

"A leader leads by example, whether he intends to or not."

~ Author Unknown

Employees will commit to a vision of a company and its culture only as much as the CEO commits to it.

The CEO might say he mentally commits to empowering employees or to creating an inspiring workplace, but unless that mental commitment leads to a change in behavior of the CEO, the program won't stick.

The CEO is the "pebble in the pond" casting ripples out that influence everyone around them. The executives and people around the CEO will mimic the CEO's behavior rather than following what the CEO says — actions speak louder than words. If the CEO doesn't truly believe in it and follow through, ultimately the employees won't either.

Consider someone who is determined to lose weight, tells others about their goal, schedules time on their calendar for exercise and healthy shopping, buys all the books and gear, but for all that, their heart isn't committed. They aren't emotionally bought in, and after a few weeks of a strong start, they weaken and become half-hearted. Things come up, they "get busy," and tell themselves, "I'll restart again next month."

If the CEO doesn't mentally and emotionally commit to CEOFlow, why should their employees do the same?

Stick to your vision for how you want your work to work for you - even through the inevitable bumps in the road that will try to knock you off your path.

You, and your mini-CEOs, can do this!

APPENDICES

APPENDIX A: Recommended Reading

For the most up to date list of recommendations,
visit www.CEOFlow.com/Resources

Authentic Business: How To Create And Run Your Perfect Business (Neil Crofts)

The Diamond Cutter: The Buddha On Managing Your Business And Your Life (Geshe Michael Roach)

Dilbert's The Joy Of Work Guide To Finding Happiness At The Expense Of Your Coworkers (Scott Adams)

Freedom Inc: Free Your Employees And Let Them Lead Your Business To Higher Productivity, Profits And Growth (Brian Carney and Isaac Getz) www. FreedomIncBook.com

The Future Of Work: How The New Order Of Business Will Shape Your Organization, Your Management Style And Your Life (Tom Malone)

The Goal: A Process of Ongoing Improvement (Eliyahu M. Goldratt)

Happiness is 9-to-5 (Alexander Kjerulf)

"Chief Happiness Officer" Blog and book site: www.PositiveSharing.com

Joy At Work: A Revolutionary Approach To Fun On The Job (Dennis Bakke of AES) www.DennisBakke.com

Let My People Go Surfing: The Education Of A Reluctant Businessman (Yvon Chouinard of Patagonia)

Maverick: The Success Story Behind the World's Most Unusual Workplace (Ricardo Semler of Semco)

Peak: How Great Companies Get Their Mojo From Maslow (Chip Conley of Joie de Vivre Hospitality) www.chipconley.com

The 4-Hour Workweek (Tim Ferriss) www.FourHourWorkweek.com

The Seven Day Weekend: Changing The Way Work Works (Ricardo Semler of Semco)

The Toyota Way: 14 Management Principles From The World's Greatest Manufacturer (Jeffrey Liker)

Wooden: A Lifetime Of Observations And Reflections Both On And Off The Court (Coach John Wooden and Steve Jamison)

Work 2.0: Building The Future, One Employee At A Time (Bill Jensen) *www.simplerwork.com*

Great Places To Work www.greatplacestowork.com

"The Great Work Blog" (www.boxofcrayons.biz/great-work) by Michael Bungay Stanier

The "Zappos Inside" Blog, www.blogs.zappos.com/blogs/inside-zappos

Worldblu (www.Worldblu.com): founded by Traci Fenton to promote the principles of democratic management and freedom organizations.

Appendix B: Semco Employee Guidelines

Semler's *The Seven Day Weekend* includes more examples of programs with titles like Rush Hour MBA, Lost in Space and Family Silverware.

"The Semco Survival Manual"

Finally, Semco has created some concrete ways it helps turn its employees into mini-CEOs. The following is a list of foundational operating principles to align how people work and to help them make their own decisions and judgment calls:

Leadership

We believe that organizational structure is required to ensure good business processes. However, only people who have respect for their followers can be leaders. Situational leadership will always be stimulated and respected.

Position

At the Semco Group, it makes no difference whether someone has a high ranking or a humble position. The most important thing is to always try to learn and teach new things.

Job Rotation

Whenever possible we rotate people: Some people change area and other people change business unit. This is another development opportunity offered by the company.

Freedom

There is no space at the Semco Group for formalities. The doors are always open and people should say what they really think, without worries or inhibitions.

Honesty

Everything at the Semco Group is based on trust. Whenever there is dishonesty, and there is always the possibility that there will be somebody dishonest, the company takes hard action.

Accusations

The company doesn't encourage people to accuse others; this should only occur when you believe you have access to concrete facts that somebody is benefiting while harming everybody else. Anonymous letters are not considered.

Gambling

No gambling of any type is permitted within the company.

Weapons and Violence

It's completely unacceptable to carry weapons inside the company. Any type of violence employed by one person against another is seen as an extremely serious event.

Unions

Unions are an important method of protecting workers. Unionization is free within the company. The Semco Group believes that constant relationships with unions are healthy for the company and the employees. The presence of union members at the company is always welcome.

You... and the Others

Based on the fact that everyone can say what they think, rumors and gossip shouldn't be stimulated. Any attempt to harm another person is looked on very seriously. Take part and speak openly about what you're thinking in order to improve things.

Sales at the Company

The entry of salespersons to deal with personal issues is only permitted when scheduled by the interested party.

Loan Sharking

Any employee lending money to another while charging interest is considered abusive, and this is dealt with by the company as a serious matter.

Discrimination

The Semco Group does not permit discrimination based on sex, color, religion, politics, etc. Everybody must have identical opportunities at the company, and the company should work to make this a reality.

Use of Authority

Many positions of the company involve the use of authority. Pressure tactics that drive people to feel afraid or any type of disrespect are considered incapable leadership and improper use of authority.

Working Hours

The Semco Group has flexible working hours where possible. This is a method of meeting the needs of each person, without harming the company.

Employee Timesheet Control

At the Semco Group, each person controls their own working hours. This is a method of transferring responsibility to each person.

Commissions

People at the Semco Group usually create commissions to deal with issues of collective interest. Take part to ensure that the commissions are active channels which effectively defend your interests, which may often not coincide with the interests of the company. Here, this conflict is seen as healthy and necessary.

Internal Promotions

At the Semco Group, people already working for the company are given preference when a new position or a promotion appears, as long as they fill the requirements for the job.

Vacations

The Semco Group does not believe that anyone is irreplaceable. Everybody must take their annual vacations, always. This is fundamental for the health of the people and the company as a whole, and no excuse is good enough to justify accumulating vacations.

Recruitment

Where there is recruitment or promotion, people in the department have the chance to interview, analyze, and take part in the decision to choose the candidate.

Retirees

We have no restrictions on active or part-time work for retirees or people of an advanced age. Nobody is too old for us; on the contrary, we believe that experience comes with age.

Everyday Participation

The Semco Group philosophy is based on active involvement and participation. Don't sit back. Have an opinion, put yourself forward as a candidate, always say what you think. Don't be just another cog in the wheel. State your opinion about everything that interests you, even if you weren't asked for it. Be active about your feelings.

Suggestions

We want everybody to participate; opinions will always be welcome and should be spontaneous. The Semco Group doesn't use and doesn't wish to suggestion box programs. Whenever there is a need or interest, we can institute campaigners that encourage specific suggestions.

Evaluation by Subordinates

Every six months you will fill in a questionnaire and say what you really think about your immediate superior. Employees are encouraged to be honest when filling in the form and afterwards, during a discussion.

Dynamism

The Semco Group is normally a company that implements major changes from time to time. Don't be scared - we think this is positive. Look at the changes without fear, and learn to see changes as typical characteristics of the Group.

Salary Policy

The Semco Group seeks to involve people in discussions regarding salary fairness for each employee. Of course, there are times when people think their salaries should be higher and the company believes it cannot pay more. What is important is to always provide an opportunity for discussions regarding this type of issue.

Strikes

The decision to take part or not in this type of event is an individual one. This is part of democracy and is respected by the company.

Personal Life

Each person's life belongs to themselves and the personal life of each person at the Semco Group is sacred. Providing it doesn't interfere with the work of the environment, the company is not interested in what each person does with their own life. The human resources area is available to provide support in any area, but the company will never get involved in people's private lives.

Former Semco Employees

Whenever anybody leaves the company, they are always welcome back. On the contrary, we have nothing against former Semco employees.

Severance

Whenever there are dismissals the company spends hours and days carefully considering the case (or cases). The company avoids dismissals as much as it can and is extremely involved in protecting justice. We must all take this line, as dismissals are very serious and must be dealt with carefully by everybody.

Occupational Safety

This isn't only a company responsibility. Keep your eyes open, always avoid accidents, use safety equipment even when it's bothersome. We cannot take risks with our health. Make a special effort along these lines, demand that the company do its part, and do not let CIPA become a pro forma commission.

Statement of Results

On a periodic basis you'll find out the results for your unit and for the company, and will be able to discuss them. Watch the results closely and ask any questions you want. There are no issues that can't be discussed. Very few companies offer this, so take advantage!

Profit Sharing Program

The Profit Sharing Program at the Semco Group is real. This is a participation in which each unit wins. Each company and the Group have its own program, according to the characteristics of each business.

Relations

In order to avoid injustice or embarrassment, close relations don' work at the same unit, workplace or with the same leader, except in special cases. In completely different and unrelated locations, there are no formal restrictions.

Hourly/Monthly Workers

At the Semco Group there is no discrimination. Here everybody is a salaried worker and everybody is treated the same.

Our Personnel

We avoid using terms like "employees," "staff," "collaborator," and similar terms. We are a team and we only have "people." This is what we call everyone who works with us. Try as hard as you can to avoid using such common terms that don't express equality.

Use of Company Resources

Don't mix company work and resources with personal services. During working hours, nobody should provide services to other people only for personal benefit. This shouldn't discourage people from using a colleague's services outside business hours and agreeing to conditions between themselves which don't involve the company.

Informality

Having a birthday party at the end of the working day or using nicknames is part of the company culture. Don't feel intimidated, and don't stick to formalities.

Pregnancy

Pregnancy is considered a time of great importance and happiness by the company. Never allow an injustice to be committed with one of our pregnant women – they deserve our respect and care.

Communication

The Semco Group and its people must communicate openly and honestly. You must be tranquil and believe what is said in company notices – demand transparency when you're in doubt.

Customer Services

This is very important. Never fail to serve a customer well; don't run away from the customer, and do for the customer exactly what you would expect if you were in their position. Be honest about deadlines, prices, and service conditions, and never promise something you can't deliver.

Pride

It's only worth working for someone you are proud of. Create this pride in the quality in what you do. Never deliver a product or service that fails to meet customer expectations, don't write a letter or communiqué that isn't honest, and don't let the company's stature fall. Always fight for your pride.

Respect to Visitors

Give our visitors all of your attention and respect. Never let anyone wait more than 5 or 10 minutes. Meet everyone with courtesy, be they a supplier, customer, or anyone else.

Appendix C: Sample CEOFlow Push/Pull Survey

	PUSH / Non-flow (Control, Politics, Surprises)	-	?	+	PULL / Flow (Trust, Transparency, Alignr
CEO enjoyment	Work is a source of stress				Work is a source of enjoyment
Inspiration	The CEO inspires employees				The employees inspire the CEO
Goal attainment	Goals are regularly missed				Goals are regularly met or exceeded
Appreciation	"No one's working hard enough" / No one's good enough (and frequently disparages work with unhelpful criticisms)				CEO appreciates everyone's work, in all forms	shares advice, feedback to improve it)
Anticipation	CEO feels angst heading to the office				CEO looks forward to getting to the office
Stress	CEO stressed, haggard				CEO stress is infrequent, passes quickly, and is
Time	The day drags				The day flows
Growth	Comes in fits and starts, spiky (when it comes at all)				Sustained, regular growth
Frustration	Clients and employees are frequently frustrating				Clients or employees rarely cause frustration
Day in a life	CEO feels like they're at the mercy of their day/schedule				CEO feels in control of their days, their work, th
"Space"	CEO feels like they never have time to think				CEO creates the 'space' for reflection, improver
Coaching	"I'm too busy to coach, they need to figure it out on their own"				CEO never too busy to focus on developing the
Board/investors	Tense, mistrustful, opaque relationships with board/investors				Transparency, trust, alignment with board/inves
Isolation	CEO often feels alone, isolated				CEO often feels embraced, welcomed, trusted
Partner / exec team	Tense, mistrustful, opaque relationships with partner(s)/execs				Transparency, trust, alignment with partner(s)/e
Forward progress	CEO feels like their people are creating as many issues as they solve, running in place				CEO's team continuously makes progress addr
Guilt	CEO feels guilty about not working harder, living unhealthily, missing family obligations...				CEO feels satisfaction, contentment
Weekends	No rest. Work piles up for weekends as "the only time I can catch up on real work"				Restful if desired. The CEO feels like it's their c work or not
Decisions	Most decisions pushed up to the CEO				CEO makes few decisions (as few as possible)

Breinigsville, PA USA
10 June 2010
239658BV00001B/29/P